Women and the Landscape of American Higher Education

Women and the Landscape of American Higher Education

Wesleyan Holiness and Pentecostal Founders

ABRAHAM RUELAS

☙PICKWICK *Publications* • Eugene, Oregon

WOMEN AND THE LANDSCAPE OF AMERICAN HIGHER EDUCATION
Wesleyan Holiness and Pentecostal Founders

Copyright © 2010 Abraham Ruelas. All rights reserved. Except for brief quotations in critical publications or reviews, no part of this book may be reproduced in any manner without prior written permission from the publisher. Write: Permissions, Wipf and Stock Publishers, 199 W. 8th Ave., Suite 3, Eugene, OR 97401.

Pickwick Publications
An Imprint of Wipf and Stock Publishers
199 W. 8th Ave., Suite 3
Eugene, OR 97401

www.wipfandstock.com

ISBN 13: 978-1-60608-869-2

Cataloging-in-Publication data:

Ruelas, Abraham.

Women and the landscape of American higher education : Wesleyan holiness and pentecostal founders / Abraham Ruelas.

xx + 166 p. ; 23 cm. Includes bibliographical references.

ISBN 13: 978-1-60608-869-2

1. Women — Education (Higher) — United States — History. 2. Pentecostalism — United States. 3. Holiness churches — United States. I. Title.

LC1752.R85 2010

Manufactured in the U.S.A.

In response to answered prayer, Hannah of the Bible presented her son at the temple, saying to Eli, the priest, "As surely as you live, my lord, I am the woman who stood beside you praying to the Lord. I prayed for this child, and the Lord granted me what I asked of Him. So now I give him to the Lord. For his whole life he will be given over to the Lord." (1 Samuel 1:26–28)

My mother, the Rev. Teresa Ruelas, is a modern-day Hannah, who because of health reasons affecting both of us, prayed a similar prayer and made a like commitment regarding me when God answered. For that I am eternally grateful.

This book is dedicated, con mucho cariño, to her.

Contents

Foreword / ix

Preface / xi

Acknowledgments / xiii

Introduction / xv

PART ONE: Wesleyan Holiness Women—Early Pioneers

1. Founded by the Philanthropy of a Woman—*Eliza Garrett* / 3
2. Her Vision, His Name—*Emma Dryer* / 8
3. "Archbishop of Deaconesses"—*Lucy Rider Meyer* / 13
4. It All Began as a One-Room Schoolhouse—*Fannie Suddarth* / 19
5. The Women of Azusa Street—*Philena B. Hadley, Mary A. Hill, M. Anna Draper, Bertha Theresa Pinkham, Matilda W. Atkinson, and Elizabeth B. Harper* / 24
6. More than Deaconesses—*Iva Vennard* / 29
7. Praying Together to Convince a Reluctant Founding President—*Bible College Prayer Circle* / 34
8. You Will Minister in This Country—*Mary Lee Cagle* / 39
9. From Tuesday Meetings to a Bible College—*Mattie Hoke* / 44
10. Mattie's Children, Mattie's School—*Mattie Mallory* / 49
11. So I'll Appoint Myself a Bishop—*Alma White* / 55
12. The General of the Kentucky Mountains—*Lela McConnell* / 60
13. Now Is the Time to Open the School—*Ruth Kerr* / 65

PART TWO: Pentecostal Women—Carrying the Torch Forward

14. Little General of the Faith Healing, Holiness, and Pentecostal Movements—*Carrie Judd Montgomery* / 73

Contents

15 Providing "Educational Fitness" to Those Called by God—*Elizabeth V. Baker* / 79

16 Following in the Footsteps of Great Grandma and Mom—*Virginia E. Moss* / 85

17 Her Tongue Talked Fluently in a Language She Had Never Learned—*Minnie Tingley Draper* / 90

18 Going Where She Thought a Man Should Go—*Nora Chambers* / 95

19 Suffering at the Hands of Revisionist Historians—*Mary Craig* / 101

20 A Gifted and Flamboyant Founder—*Aimee Semple McPherson* / 107

21 Operating by the Faith Principle—*Christine Amelia Gibson* / 112

22 Affirming Indigenous Leadership . . . Almost—*Alice Luce* / 117

23 Fulfilling the Vision of the Founder—*Mary Keith* / 122

24 Answering God's Call in the Middle of the Detroit River—*Bebe Patten* / 128

25 That They May Reach Their Own Tribes in the Native Language—*Alta Washburn* / 133

26 The Mantle of God Is upon Her—*Violet Kiteley* / 139

27 She Guarded the Secret in Her Heart—*Freda Lindsay* / 144

Conclusion / 149

Appendix: Timeline of Wesleyan Holiness and Pentecostal Founders / 151

Bibliography / 155

Index / 163

Foreword

THE REVIVAL OF THE women's movement in American society in the latter decades of the twentieth century spawned an interest in the history of women's involvement in the church. Books on women evangelists, women pastors, and women missionaries have appeared documenting their activities. This has been especially true in the Wesleyan Holiness and Pentecostal movements, where women initially played significant roles disseminating the gospel message. Professor Ruelas has made a valuable contribution to this literature by systematically documenting the prominent place of Wesleyan Holiness and Pentecostal women in establishing Christian academic institutions between 1855 and 1970 to prepare individuals for ministry. While stereotypes of women involved in education might restrict them to the role of teachers, he has put that limitation to rest by focusing on women whose calling led them to establish Bible training schools and institutes.

Professor Ruelas is the first scholar who has undertaken the difficult task of uncovering a past that, in many cases, has never been explored. One of the challenges of researching this topic is the scarcity of materials available. While we may wish for more details, often they are just not to be found. Plowing new ground in the field of women's religious history, his research led him to archives to examine obscure school documents. In one instance, the name of a woman who founded a school had been deleted from subsequent histories of the institution. It was clear from early school records that the woman was, in fact, the founder. In another case, the credit went to a denominational leader rather than to the group of women who had prayed and raised money for a school.

While several of the women included here are well known, most are being introduced for the first time. They make a considerable addition to "the great cloud of witnesses" (Heb 12:1) who have gone before us. They add to a usable past, in this case, as founders and leaders of religious schools. In most instances, these women's work did not end with estab-

Foreword

lishing a school. Many served as principals or presidents shouldering all the responsibilities, including fundraising. They either operated on the faith line, trusting God to provide all their needs, or solicited supporters to finance their schools. Endowments to serve as backup to meet financial needs were unheard of in their time. Expectations for student contributions were minimal. In one case, students paid $20 a year for tuition and $5 a week for room and board. Six schools out of 111 in the Council for Christian Colleges & Universities currently have women presidents. In light of the precedent of women presidents, it should not be surprising that all six schools are affiliated with the Wesleyan Holiness or Pentecostal movements (Asbury College, Warner Pacific College, Messiah College, Houghton College, Eastern Nazarene College, and Vanguard University of Southern California).

Professor Ruelas's research further puts to rest the mistaken notion that Wesleyan Holiness and Pentecostal believers were not interested in intellectual pursuits. While the designation of "Bible training school" or "institute" may sound like the schools had a narrow agenda, a look at their curricula offers a different perspective. Besides classes in Bible and theology, students studied subjects such as ancient and modern history, rhetoric, Greek, English, math, science, music, economics, Latin, and German.

Professor Ruelas has contributed significantly to women's studies by researching the ministries of Wesleyan Holiness and Pentecostal women who founded academic institutions. In many cases, the Bible training schools and institutes they established became the foundation for Christian liberal arts colleges that are still in operation today. Several examples of schools that trace their roots to these schools are Garrett Evangelical Theological Seminary, Azusa Pacific University, Moody Bible Institute, Bethany University, Latin American Bible Institute, Patten University, and Zion Bible College.

Women and the Landscape of American Higher Education is a great testimony to the women who answered God's call to educate people so that they would be qualified to fulfill their own calling to ministry.

Susie C. Stanley
Professor of Historical Theology
Messiah College
Founder and Executive Director of Wesleyan/Holiness Women Clergy, Intl. (1991–2006)

Preface

THE GENESIS OF THIS book begins in the classroom of my Sunday school teacher Gloria Arias. She is a very dedicated Christian woman who poured her love into every child she taught.

During Vacation Bible School, constructing crafts under the tutelage of my mother, Rev. Teresa Ruelas, was always an exciting time. The crafts were always "a cut above," and among them were ships made with real seashells, and corn tortillas presses. She was inspired to get involved in this important ministry as a young woman through a mailing from Ms. Alice Luce, one of the founders included in this book.

During my adolescent years in Templo Betania of Fremont, California, Rev. Julia Valentin was the first woman I ever heard preach. She combined Pentecostal fire with deep Bible knowledge and a great compassion for souls.

This journey rounds the next corner when, in 1970, I enrolled at Patten Bible College (now Patten University). There I encountered a dynamo—Dr. Bebe Patten, the founder of the school. She was also preacher, pastor, teacher, administrator, songwriter, author, and a radio and television personality. For thirty-four years she mentored me as I became involved in various aspects of her ministry—not unlike how the Apostle Paul guided Timothy.

Like so many women included in this book, founding a Christian college was but one of the achievements of Dr. Patten. Along with the Oakland Bible Institute (the university's original name), she founded Christian Cathedral Church, Patten Academy of Christian Education (K–12), and the Christian Evangelical Churches of America, Inc., a Pentecostal Holiness denomination.

The theme of the 2009 Society for Pentecostal Studies conference was "What does the Spirit have to say through the Academy?" Since Wesleyan Holiness and Pentecostalism are the foundations of my faith journey, I set out to put together the "great cloud of [women] witnesses" (Heb 12:1) from these two faith traditions who founded Christian colleges. I now get to live the dream of developing the message of that conference paper into a published book.

My intent in writing this book is to pay tribute to women, who, like Dr. Patten, succeeded in the face of societal, cultural, and religious biases and restrictions in answering the call to ministry that God had placed in their hearts. Even if many of the Christian higher education institutions that these women founded no longer exist, or have been merged into other institutions, it is of paramount importance to honor their life journeys in the service of God.

Acknowledgments

A SPECIAL TRIBUTE IS due to two important mentors in my pursuit of a greater understanding of women in ministry, the nexus of my academic research and advocacy: Dr. Susie Stanley of Messiah College, in the area of Wesleyan Holiness women; and Dr. Kimberly Alexander of the Pentecostal Theological Seminary, in the area of women in Pentecostalism.

A book like this would not be possible without the assistance of helpful individuals, including the staff members of the archive departments of Azusa Pacific University, Bethany University, Life Pacific College, Moody Bible Institute, the Church of the Nazarene, Patten University, Point Loma Nazarene University, Southern Nazarene University, Westmont College, the president's offices of Kentucky Mountain Bible College and Shiloh Bible College, the alumni office of Zion Bible College, The New and Living Way Publishing Company (Keith Dominion), the Dixon Pentecostal Research Center, and the Flower Pentecostal Heritage Center.

The journey of writing of this book was as much spiritual as it was academic. The friendship, prayers, and guidance of my pastor, Rev. Tobey Montgomery, were essential in celebrating the victories and overcoming the challenges encountered along the way. Undergirding the focus and persistence that was necessary for this undertaking were the constant prayers of the Christian Cathedral Prayer Meeting group and the Patten community.

In reading the drafts of the manuscript, Dr. Ken Romines contributed important insights from his background in historiography and his knowledge of a number of denominational histories. Al Carlos Hernandez, professor of communication and online columnist, provided important critiques as to the writing of the biographical sketches.

Special appreciation is due to my very close friend, life companion, and wife, Patricia, for her support, prayers, patience, and for taking me away from my work for cappuccinos, frozen yogurt, and short vacations so that I could be renewed both mentally and spiritually for this important task.

Introduction

During the beginning stages of the American experience, John Winthrop, governor of the Massachusetts Bay Colony, declared that Mistress Anne Hopkins, wife of the Connecticut governor, had gone insane because she had stretched beyond a woman's mental capacities by thinking about things theological.[1] He wrote that Mistress Hopkins had "lost her wits 'by occasion of her givinge her selfe whooly to reading & writinge, & had written many bookes: her husband beinge very lovinge and tender of her, was lothe to greive her, but sawe his error when it ws to late: for if she had attended her househould affaires, & suche thinges as belonge to women, & not gone out of her waye and callinge, to meddle in suche things as are proper for men, whose mindes are stronger: she had kept her wittes, & might have improved them usefully and honorably in the place God sett her.'"[2]

Given that women in the late 1700s and the early 1800s were viewed as intellectually weaker than men, envisioning that women would be instrumental in founding institutions of higher education in the nineteenth and twentieth centuries was out of the question. Yet, women came to play, and continue to play, a key role in educational life of the United States at all levels: preschool, elementary, middle and high school, college, university, and seminary.

Early educational opportunities provided to women were "academies" intended specifically for women, with a curriculum of French, music, drawing, sewing, and parlor etiquette. The focus was on domesticity. Upper-middle-class women were to serve as adornments within the home for display by their husbands. By 1850, however, this view of women and education had changed as Protestant Americans embraced a post-millennial paradigm. According to this interpretation of Scripture the second coming of Christ would occur after the Millennium, during

---

1. Tucker and Liefeld. *Daughters of the Church,* 216.
2. Ulrich, "John Winthrop's City of Women," 9.

Introduction

which the kingdom of God would be established. It was therefore the duty of Christians to perfect society in preparation for this time of Christian dominance and prosperity.

"Throughout the 1830s, 1840s, and 1850s, America's evangelical denominations were competing furiously with one another to give their daughters the same intellectual training as sons. With passionate engagement they built female seminaries and encouraged their members to build them."[3] Traditional women's education, which had previously consisted of private education and boarding schools, was being replaced with more of an institutional approach, complete with large classical buildings that housed classrooms (with desks aligned in rows), dormitory rooms, chapels, and dining halls. Women in the seminaries mastered "masculine studies" such as Latin, Greek, mathematics, science, and metaphysics. However, the goal of these seminaries was not to move women beyond the sphere of domesticity.

"The concept of messianic motherhood, yoked forces with the millennialism of evangelical religion" to provide "a powerful impetus for female education."[4] Since Protestant America was building God's kingdom on earth, it was vitally important to maximize the usefulness of wives and mothers for the effort. At the time, women were viewed as morally superior to men, and so it was thought their ethical influence combined with their intellectual prowess would enable them to make the home a place to nurture ideal individuals for the construction of the kingdom of God on earth. The aim of female education was more than learning by rote, but instead developing in women a disciplined intellect and critical thinking skills.[5]

Ironically, the education that was developed to maximize women's domestic frame of mind enabled them to look beyond their designated sphere of hearth and home. The female seminaries entered the educational landscape at a time when there was a growing segment of single women. These schools prepared women for the field of teaching. Within society at the time, single status among women was gaining respectability, and the social norm shifted somewhat away from the expectation for women to marry at a young age. Employment as teachers gave women more control

---

3. Sweet, "Female Seminary Movement," 41.
4. Ibid., 44.
5. McGill, "Present Age," 7.

over their economic future, although female teachers were paid at a lower scale than their male counterparts.

Theologically, "evangelicalism's stress on the individual soul, standing before God in a state of solitary accountability, generated an egalitarianism that worked to the advantage of women."[6] A person's "usefulness" in the kingdom of God, whether male or female, was seen as the end goal of one's life. The paradox, however, was that while men pursued education not to become better husbands and fathers but to learn a profession, the end goal of women's educational opportunities was to make them better in their roles as wives and mothers. As "a professor of Greek and Latin informed a group of seminary students in 1847," the end goal was "the 'formation of a perfect mind' in a 'perfect woman,' . . . that required first of all a well-cultivated intellect followed by a finely tuned moral nature, deep piety and graceful manners."[7] Even among American blacks in post-slavery times, this was a consistent theme. Reverend Anthony Binga, a Virginia minister, argued for creating educational opportunities for black women as he "considered an uneducated mother, no matter how devoted to her children, unprepared to meet the demands of the age."[8]

Ultimately, women's educational opportunities were not intended to move women from the domain of the home to the "public" sphere. Their purpose was to strengthen the "influence" rather than the power of the "hand that rocked the cradle." Within the framework of a postmillennial worldview, female education was seen as a means of world regeneration through women's work in the home. However, the liberal education provided by female seminaries enabled women—primarily single women—to move from domesticity into the public role of teaching.

Although primarily focused on the education of children, these women teachers fulfilled a religious role as well. The sponsoring boards of frontier teachers required of them (1) a testimony of personal conversion, and (2) a letter of support from their ministers.[9] Pioneer teachers founded Sunday schools as well as secular schools, and in the absence of permanent churches, because of their literacy they took on religious responsibilities such as leading public prayer.

---

6. Sweet, "Female Seminary Movement," 48.
7. Ibid., 49.
8. Higgenbotham, *Righteous Discontent*, 23.
9. Lindley, *"You Have Stept Out of Your Place,"* 93.

Introduction

In the work of evangelizing the American West, Catherine Beecher believed that the work of teachers was complementary with that of ministers, such as her famous revivalist father, Lyman. She argued "that teachers are needed as much as ministers, that teachers' institutions are as important as colleges, that it is as necessary to educate and send forth 'poor and pious women' to teach, as it is 'poor and pious young men' to preach."[10]

Back home, women had begun founding schools, primarily women's seminaries. Emma Willard founded Troy Seminary in 1821, Mary Lyon founded Mount Holyoke Female Seminary in 1837, and Catherine Beecher founded Hartford Female Seminary in 1828. These efforts were based on an interweaving of the goals of creating educational opportunities for women and broadening the influence of the Christian faith. "Religion, specifically Protestantism of the Second Great Awakening, was an intrinsic part of both sides of early female education, the traditional and potentially radical. Willard, Lyon and Beecher were all devout Christians, and they used explicit religious justifications openly in their appeals for support. Moreover, religion was a persuasive influence at their schools, both as part of the regular curriculum and in the periodic revivals they fostered on campus."[11]

Women had gone through a major revolution in the world of American education. First, they were seen as genetically having less intellectual acumen than men. In pre-Revolutionary times their literacy rate was less than half that of men. However, with the shift in how women and their intellect were viewed came a shift in intellectual opportunities, enabling the literacy rate of women to equal that of men by 1850.[12] However, their education was geared to keeping women within the sphere of domesticity. The education women were engaged in was either to prepare children and youth for the coming kingdom of God on earth, or to prepare each other for the domestic roles of wife and mother.

An early 1800s-era corollary of this expansion of educational opportunities for women was the birth and expansion of the Holiness revival. The year 1835 marked a significant point in this movement with the birth of the Tuesday meetings established by Sarah Worral Langford.[13] At these

---

10. Beecher, *Duty of American Women*, 61–62.
11. Lindley, "You Have Stept Out of Your Place," 92.
12. Sklar, "Founding of Mt. Holyoke College," 179–80.
13. Dieter, *Holiness Revival*, 23.

Introduction

meetings Christians pursued and nurtured the experience of sanctification (also known as "Christian perfection" and the "second blessing"), a complete surrender to God's will that was most often accompanied by a sense of inner peace. Soon thereafter Ms. Langford moved away, and this work was continued by her sister Phoebe Palmer. Palmer, the recognized founder of the Holiness movement, expanded the theological framework of the revival with her "altar theology."[14] A believer would only be able to experience entire sanctification when the individual's all was placed on the altar that is Jesus Christ.

The significance of sanctification and altar theology was the liberating impact it had on women and their relationship to the "women's" and "public" spheres. "The doctrine of sanctification played a major role in transforming Wesleyan/Holiness women's understanding of self, making it possible for them to transcend the constructions of self imposed on them by various forces in society."[15]

Women within this faith tradition were thus empowered to enter the "public" spheres of preaching, previous the domain of men only. They also did the "public" work of founding churches, missionary efforts, social relief ministries, denominations, and ultimately educational institutions for the training of ministers for evangelistic work both at home and abroad. The impetus of this work occurred in the mid to late 1800s as Wesleyan Holiness women worked diligently to gain souls for the kingdom of God and transform society to God's ideal.

At the beginning of the twentieth century a new force would enable women to further demonstrate their equality in the work of the Lord. In 1901, the Pentecostal movement was ushered in when Agnes Nevada Ozman became the first person in the modern era to speak in tongues.[16] The promise and fulfillment of equal empowerment of men and women for service by the Holy Spirit sent individuals throughout the world to further the kingdom of God.

However, this "kingdom" was now viewed through a different lens, as there was a theological shift from postmillennialism to premillennialism. Optimism turned to pessimism and hope became despair and urgency because of the increasingly sinful condition of humanity and the immi-

---

14. Ibid., 23–24.
15. Stanley, *Holy Boldness*, 5.
16. Blumhofer, "Agnes Nevada Ozman," 952.

Introduction

nent return of Christ for his saints. Based on a literal interpretation of Revelation 20:1–10, the return of Christ would precede the thousand-year reign of Christ known as the Millennium. The motivation for Christian ministry was no longer the transformation of society into the kingdom of God on earth. Instead society was viewed as being on a consistent trajectory of decay and increasing evil until Christ returned to redeem his church. It was therefore of utmost importance to reach as many souls with the message of the gospel before the second coming of Christ.

Regardless of whether the motivation had a post- or premillennial foundation, there existed a need to establish schools to train ministers for the task of ministry—evangelistic, missional, pastoral—and women were central to the process of founding these schools. The focus of this study is on women from the Wesleyan Holiness and Pentecostal traditions who founded these Christian institutions of higher education. Following are the stories of these women who had, from society's perspective, stepped out of *their* place to claim *a significant place* in the history of American higher education.

PART ONE

Wesleyan Holiness Women
Early Pioneers

1

Founded by the Philanthropy of a Woman

Eliza Garrett

"The name of Eliza Garrett will be honored while the world endures. As time shall develop the good results and the far-reaching influence of the institution founded by her munificence, it will be ranked by faithful historians with the names of Brown and Girard, Harvard and Yale. It will be singular in American history as that of the first female in our country who has attained so distinguished a rank by an act of Christian philanthropy."[1]

Thus begins an 1861 biographical sketch of the woman born Eliza Clark into a strong Christian home in Newburgh, New York. Her life journey would take her from the family farm in Newburgh to various American cities before she and her husband would settle down in the city of Chicago during its nascent years. It would be in this city that Eliza would make her mark in the world.

As a child, Eliza's Presbyterian parents instilled in her the value that that "none of us liveth to himself, and no man dieth to himself."[2] Although she was raised in a Presbyterian home, Eliza was thought to have become a probationary member of the Methodist Episcopal Church.

At the age of twenty, Eliza married Augustus Garrett, and after four years of unsuccessfully trying to make a living as farmers, the couple set out west. It was not an easy decision, as noted in Augustus' description of the move: "I left my country, the land that gave me birth . . . that my Father

---

1. Clark, "Mrs. Eliza Garrett," 201.
2. Stevens, *Women of Methodism*, 263.

and my Mother inherited for a long while. With all I left behind my aged Father and Mother and so did my wife which caused her to weep for many salutary hours to seek an asylum in a new country amongst strangers."[3]

What followed was six years of unsuccessful business ventures, and parental grief due to the death of their three children. Eliza and Augustus first settled in Cincinnati where Augustus' business ventures landed him in court, being sued by his creditors. Having paid his debt, the couple traveled south via the Mississippi River. En route, their four-year-old daughter Imogene died of cholera and was buried in an unmarked grave along the river. In Natchitoches, Texas, a second child, Charles, also died. Their third child, John, died shortly after birth a few years later when Augustus and Eliza lived in Chicago.

Augustus next tried his business acumen in the city of New Orleans, a city of more than 30,000 that was attracting entrepreneurs seeking to get rich. Unfortunately, Augustus was a total failure, and as a result he sent Eliza to live with her family until he could achieve some sense of economic stability.

Augustus arrived in Chicago in 1834 still in debt from a previous business venture. However, he soon found success in real estate speculation, and by the following year his real estate sales were valued at $1,800,000. He also sold marine and fire insurance and was part owner in Seaman and Garrett, a company that brokered the purchase of goods from New York. Having achieved financial solvency at last, Augustus sent for Eliza to join him.

In 1839 Eliza and her husband Augustus were converted under the preaching of Peter Borein, pastor of the Clark Street Methodist Episcopal Church (now Chicago Temple). Because of this experience Eliza began a deeply devoted life in service to her Savior. "Methodism found in her a devoted disciple, reverent in attendance upon the sanctuary, punctual in her place at the prayer meeting, edifying by her testimony in the class meeting, and abundant in her acts of charity."[4] Augustus, however, struggled with his Christian walk and went through as many as twenty conversion experiences during the remaining nine years of his life.

Eliza also learned that her pastor, Peter Borein, suffered much regret because he lacked formal education. Born to illiterate farmers in

---

3. Garrett, letter to Jerry Clark, 1.
4. Buoy, *Representative Women of Methodism*, 346.

Founded by the Philanthropy of a Woman

Tennessee, Borein was converted and received his call to ministry as a teenager. Although having to overcome having not even learned the alphabet, he succeeded as a student in his two years at Jacksonville College. As a preacher he captivated audiences with his homiletics, enthusiasm, and ability to craft word pictures to dramatize truths from the Bible. Self-taught in Hebrew, Borein expressed his own frustration both at not receiving formal education as a minister and at the lack of a school where such education could take place. Rectifying this situation for future ministers became a central goal of Eliza's life.

Having established himself among the city's wealthy elite, Augustus was elected mayor of Chicago in 1843, and after a year out of office was reelected in 1845. As mayor, he ensured that there were public vaccinations available to combat the cholera and smallpox epidemics plaguing the nation at the time. He also made sure that the Chicago battalion had the financial support it needed to fight in the Mexican-American War.

Following the end of his political career it seemed that Augustus became aware of his moral lapses and discussed with Eliza how he might contribute to founding of a Christian institution. Although he was reluctant to give money to an existing Methodist school, he was persuaded by Grant Goodrich, his lawyer, to invest money in the Rock River Seminary. When he discovered that his money was a donation rather than an investment in a profit-making venture, he became incensed and described himself as being "falsely and scandalously used." He then demanded his money back.

Shortly after his death in 1848, Eliza wrote in a letter to friends regarding Augustus, "I had prayed and hoped that he would live to do some little good in the world before he should have been called up to give his account ... I am sorry that he has left nothing satisfactory in regard to the future."[5]

In his will, Augustus left Eliza half his fortune. His will also included an elaborate system for paying off his debts, and an allowance of $1,000 a year for Eliza to live on until all the debts were resolved. In order to maximize the amount of money in the estate that would be available for the establishment of the biblical institute she had in mind, Eliza budgeted herself $400 a year instead. Of that amount she gave away $200 to benevolence work and lived with friends so she could sustain herself on the re-

---

5. Fisher, "Eliza Garrett," 55.

maining amount. Her ultimate dream was to establish a school that would forever offer tuition-free ministerial education to qualified students.

In addition to her concern for establishing a school for male clergy, she also wanted to expand educational opportunities for women. Although there was growing interest in providing higher education to women in other parts of the country, there was no such school in the Chicago area. In 1853 she wrote a will leaving the majority of her estate for the establishment of a biblical institute, with a provision that if there were monies left over they be used for the establishment of a women's college.

Given that Eliza had provided sufficient financial backing for the venture, on December 26, 1853, "The Friends of Biblical Learning" held its first official meeting to explore the possibility of establishing such an institute. At the meeting, the decision whether to proceed with the institute fell to John Clark, pastor of the Clark Street Church; Grant Goodrich, attorney for the estate; minister Philo Judson; businessman Orrington Lun; and John Evans, an influential Methodist layperson after whom the city of Evanston was named. However, they worked "under the shadow of a woman" because without the financial backing provided by Eliza "all their talk would probably brought no action."[6] Anticipating resistance from the church concerning the effect learning would have on its pastors, "The Friends of Biblical Learning" moved to make the biblical institute a reality as soon as possible. At the 1854 General Conference of the Methodist Episcopal Church, hesitancy to authorize the establishment of the biblical institute was overcome because of the financial backing provided by Eliza Garrett.

Thus the Garrett Biblical Institute (GBI) was born in Evanston, Illinois, with four students and three faculty members. Evanston, considered to be a Methodist town, was a significant city for GBI to call home. It was the home of Francis Willard, and to this day it is the headquarters of the Woman's Christian Temperance Union. Currently, a number of United Methodist agencies also have their headquarters there.

The inauguration ceremony of the Garrett Biblical Institute was the only event that Eliza ever attended. She died shortly afterward on November 18, 1855. Her final words were, "Bless the Lord, O my soul, and forget not his benefits."[7]

---

6. Norwood, *Dawn to Midday at Garrett*, 11.
7. Fisher, "Eliza Garrett," 51.

Founded by the Philanthropy of a Woman

Although no separate institute for women was ever established, women began attending GBI in 1874. Additionally, the Chicago Training School for City, Home and Foreign Missions, founded by Lucy Rider Meyer, was later incorporated into GBI. Garrett was an example to other women who likewise, through their philanthropic efforts, helped develop the Garrett Bible Institute and later the seminary. When Dempster Hall was enlarged, women's societies furnished the rooms. The $50,000 construction cost of building a larger dorm was raised by the American Methodist Ladies Centenary Association. Appropriately this dorm was named Heck Hall in honor of Barbara Heck, the founder of American Methodism.

Dr. Nellie Huger Ebersake had long dreamed of founding an educational center for sacred music, but, because of her age and health, knew that she could not found the institution herself. Instead, she contributed $250,000 for the establishment of the Nellie Huger Ebersake Endowment in Church Music at Garrett-Evangelical Theological Seminary. Truly, "no other theological seminary has been more deeply influenced by the active participation of women."[8]

In addition to being a noted Methodist institution of higher education institute, GBI would also have a significant place in the Holiness movement. Randolph Foster, an influential Holiness advocate, made an impact in the movement of Methodist perfectionism both through his book *Christian Purity* and his teaching at GBI.[9] As part of a series of conference camps, Phoebe Palmer and her husband held a three-week revival at GBI in 1876. During this revival, "Frances Willard, future president of the Woman's Christian Temperance Union, professed sanctification."[10]

Eliza's legacy continues to this day. "She linked her name to posterity, and, in honoring her Church, lives today in its highest ministry."[11] Eliza's vision of founding an institution of higher education for the training of ministers "established a tradition for women (and men) in later years to emulate" providing "opportunities for growth to those who will serve the church."[12]

---

8. Norwood, *Dawn to Midday*, 11.
9. Dieter, *Holiness Revival*, 44.
10. Smith, *Called unto Holiness*, 15.
11. Buoy, *Representative Women of Methodism*, 344.
12. Fisher, "Eliza Garrett," 54.

2

Her Vision, His Name

Emma Dryer

EMELINE "EMMA" WAS BORN to John and Lucinda in 1835 while they were visiting in Massachusetts. Unfortunately, in her early childhood, John and Lucinda died and Emma's upbringing was entrusted to another. Unexpectedly orphaned, Emeline "Emma" Dryer was soon adopted by her aunt in New York.

Her aunt made sure that Emma developed a strong foundation in Bible knowledge and made the most of her education. Emma accepted the Lord as a youngster and faithfully attended church. She graduated with highest honors from New York's first college for women, the Ingham University at LeRoy. After graduation she taught at the Knoxville Female College until the Civil War. Emma was then employed as an elementary school teacher for a few years before serving as preceptress (dean of women) and teaching grammar and drawing at the Illinois State Normal University from 1864 to 1870.[1]

In 1870, at the age of 35, Emma contracted typhoid fever and was not expected to live. She was miraculously healed however, and through this experience she received a revelation that God was calling her to full-time ministry. She readily made the decision to leave a well-paid position in education to engage in unsalaried ministerial work in Chicago.

During the late 1880s, Chicago was a city impacted by significant changes brought about by rapid industrial growth and a population explosion because of the need for factory workers. Most were immigrants

---

1. Harmon, "Women Building Chicago," 1.

from Europe seeking a better life in America. Chicago, the city Emma settled in, had become a stark contrast between the opulence of the rich and abject poverty of the tenement dwellers.

Once in Chicago, Emma began attending services at the First Methodist Episcopal Church, where Rev. William H. Daniels was pastor. She soon became friends with Daniels and his wife. She also became acquainted with Rev. William J. Eerdman, who convinced her of the doctrine of premillenialism, according to which the second coming of Christ will occur before he establishes his thousand-year reign on earth. Embracing this doctrine became the driving force in her evangelism and missionary work; it was imperative for Emma to bring as many souls as possible to the saving knowledge of Christ before his return. Still, she did not abandon her postmillennial ideal that education was central to the spiritual development of individuals and the transformation of society.

Emma visited local jails with Sarah Clarke, the cofounder of the Pacific Garden Mission, to share the Scriptures with the inmates. She also evangelized prostitutes. Her involvement in relief work after the 1871 Chicago fire led to her appointment as superintendent of the Women's Auxiliary of the YMCA (later known as the YWCA). During the summer of that year, Emma was introduced by two missionary friends, Mrs. Sarah Cleveland and Miss Alice Miller, to Dwight L. Moody, one of the most prominent revivalists of America's Third Great Awakening. Emma impressed Moody as "a woman of high intelligence, with superb teaching skills and a deep, practical knowledge of Scripture."[2]

In May of 1873, Emma was hired by the Chicago Avenue Church (formerly the Illinois Street Church) as a Bible teacher and to direct its Bible school. While employed there, on more than one occasion she expressed to Rev. Charles A. Blanchard, then pastor of the church, her desire to establish a Bible institute that would train individuals for ministerial work.

During the winter of that year, Moody persuaded Emma to join with his ministry and direct the Bible Work of Chicago (BWC), an organization founded to train urban workers to lead Bible studies and prayer in neighborhoods, and distribute Bibles for the Chicago Bible Society. The initiation of BWC's work was made possible through a $500 contribution by Mrs. Nancy "Nettie" Fowler McCormick, the wife of Cyrus Hall

---

2. "Emeline Dryer: Christian Educator," 1.

McCormick Sr., founder of McCormick Reaper Works. Nettie became a lifelong philanthropist in her own right.

The day-to-day operations of the BWC were the responsibility of the Chicago Bible Society, a branch of the American Bible Society. By 1878, seventeen people were ministering under Emma's supervision. Pastors, evangelists, physicians and others were brought in to provide instruction to the workers.

The BWC and other urban missions work provided opportunities for evangelical women in public ministry. Although their lives were prescribed by the two-sphere paradigm—home for women, "public" arena for men—urban work enabled women to step into the "public" sphere. Whether serving in ministry or in social agencies, they could do so with their respectability intact because of the virtue ascribed to women by society. In addition, their efforts were geared towards bringing morality to the chaos that was the urban city. For Emma, this work enabled her to envision "an all-female institution where women could live together while they were taught and supported in ministry."[3]

Having captured this vision as her own, Emma consistently lobbied Moody to establish such a school. However, because his focus was on his own evangelistic work, he was resistant to the idea. Her visit in 1879 to the deaconess program in Midmay, England, provided her a model for ministry that she transposed to her work in Chicago. Female workers were encouraged to live in the neighborhoods where they ministered through leading home prayer meetings, scripture reading, and establishment of sewing schools.

Using the Midmay program as a model, the BWC sponsored annual May Institutes starting in 1883, which were held in the YMCA building at 150 Madison Street. The intent of these institutes was to train individuals as evangelists, pastoral helpers, missionaries, and other types of Christian workers. The school started with fifty students and expanded to seventy-five in the winter of 1884–85. The enthusiasm with which the May Institutes were received convinced Moody to establish the school Dryer had lobbied for. The success of the institutes also persuaded Moody's trustees to buy an empty lot so that a school could be established.

Moody signaled his support for the school by referring to its potential to equip males for ministry during a meeting in which the concept

---

3. Joiner, *Sin in the City*, 45.

of the training school was discussed. "I tell you what I want, and what I have on my heart, I believe that we have got to have gapmen: men to stand between the laity and the ministers; men who are trained to do city mission work. Take men that have the gifts and train them for the work of reaching the people." The comment was significant because up to this point the majority of the work Moody envisioned was already being accomplished by women.

Finally in agreement about the need to establish the school, there remained distinct areas of disagreement between Moody and Emma. One was doctrinal, as Dryer believed in divine healing and Moody did not. Another disagreement was over which emphasis should drive the BWC—evangelism or education. Moody's life centered on evangelism, and from his perspective, educational efforts took away from evangelistic work.

Also, Moody did not agree with Dryer's engagement in social issues, especially with the temperance movement. His opposition to temperance work was such that he made her break her ties with the WTCU as a condition for him returning to Chicago. She very reluctantly agreed because she ultimately believed that God wanted Moody in Chicago. Finally, each had their own vision for the school that would become Moody Bible Institute—she a school for women, he a coed school.

Ultimately, the conflict between Moody and Dryer illustrated the tension inherent in evangelical norms regarding gender at that time. "On the one hand, their vision for urban ministry promoted female initiative and independence. On the other, evangelical ideals of submission and acquiescence constantly constrained female missionaries. Urban work entailed men being in charge. Yet men desperately needed the expertise, footwork, and familial beachheads in urban neighborhoods that women workers could provide."[4]

When the Chicago Evangelism Society (CES) was formed in 1883, Dryer and her supporters took umbrage with the fact that the women's ministry ("Ladies Council") was relegated to the bylaws rather than the constitution of the organization. Specifically, Nettie McCormick "saw the diminished constitutional status of the women's program as undermining the legitimacy of the newly formed institute, and, perhaps more importantly, as a betrayal of Emma Dryer's life goal."[5]

---

4. Ibid.
5. Ibid., 58.

McCormick withdrew her financial backing of the school and Moody his support for establishing the institute. Ultimately, another Emma, Moody's wife, brought about a reconciliation, and in 1888 the BWS established by Emma was incorporated into the Chicago Evangelism Society. Although, she wrote shortly thereafter, "I certainly am ready to unite the work and the Board and all concerned," a fractious time would follow in what Moody's supporters saw as a power struggle between Moody and Emma.

Emma was perceived as not coming sufficiently into submission to Moody's leadership, and so her abilities to lead and work cooperatively in ministry were called into question. Mrs. T. W. Harvey, wife of the spokesperson for the board, wrote, "We feel that quite outside the differences in method between Mr. Moody and Miss Dryer, Miss Dryer lacks the breadth and sympathy to mother an extensive establishment, and that her experience in life has narrowed and set her convictions to such an extent that it is quite out of the question that she work with a Board, unless she is recognized as the absolute ruler."[6]

Although Emma was initially selected to head the Ladies Council, she was ultimately forced out of the very school she had lobbied for and had worked so hard to have established. In the face of increasing board opposition to her leadership role, Emma refused to resign. As a result, at the October 1888 board meeting, with Emma present, the board selected Mrs. Capron, a missionary from India, to replace her.

Emma and the Bible Work of Chicago both became disassociated with the CES, and Dryer continued in urban ministry. The 1901 annual report of the Chicago Bible Society showed that Emma and her staff had made 13,324 home visits, held or spoke at 1306 meetings, and had recruited 140 persons to Bible study sessions.[7] The McCormick family continued to provide her with financial support for the rest of her life.

Within the context of the Third Great Awakening revival era, Emma, like her female contemporaries, was encouraged to utilize her female initiative and independence as long as it did not challenge male leadership. Emma continued to effectively minister, undeterred by challenges and setbacks to both her vision and leadership roles. In doing so, she earned her place of recognition alongside Dwight Moody, Charles Finney, and Billie Sunday, the most noted revivalists of her time.

6. Harvey, letter to Nettie McCormick.
7. Mulliken, "Sixty-Second Report."

3

"Archbishop of Deaconesses"

Lucy Rider Meyer

The rebirth of the order of deaconesses is credited to Theodore Fliedner of Germany. During a trip to England he was impressed by the practical, philanthropic work in prisons and work houses led by Elizabeth Fry. He returned to his native Germany, and established the Kaiserwerth Deaconesses. These deaconesses were to fulfill a three-fold ministry. According to Fliedner, "we must be servants in a three fold way, servants of the Lord Jesus, servants of the sick and poor for Jesus' sake, and servants of each other."[1]

The start of the Kaiserwerth Deaconesses was humble, beginning with one woman who lived in the "garden house" of his home. As more women came forward to serve, a larger place was secured for their living quarters. In 1936, Fliedner converted half of his home into a hospital and soon he had his first volunteer prepared to learn nursing. Although his work was initially opposed by both Protestants and Roman Catholics, the need it filled for poor and rich, especially in the area of medical care, led to its acceptance. With the backing and financial support of the king and queen of Germany, Fliedner was able to add to his ministry, schools, reformatories, orphanages, lunatic asylums and schools to train servant girls.

In addition to restoring the order of deaconesses, Fliedner provided a model that the Methodist Episcopal Church was to follow, both in Europe and in the America. During the latter half of the nineteenth

---

1. Meyer, *Deaconesses*, 36.

century this work was especially important, as the United States was experiencing a rapid growth within its urban centers brought on by massive immigration. This influx led to major problems of overcrowding, illness, and social problems as most of the immigrants were unskilled, illiterate, and foreign-speaking. The church responded by developing a variety of medical, employment, cultural, and intervention programs.

Mission society work within the Methodist Church was based on the notion of "evangelical domesticity," which adhered to the fundamental belief that "the world could be made perfect through the redemptive power of women." Based on their "moral superiority," women were enlisted as "crusaders [who] went out into the community as evangelists for the home."[2] As an office of the church, scripturally the rationale drew its foundation from the "Greek word Diakonos—of which the English word Deaconess is the translation—[which] has at the heart the meaning, prompt and helpful service."[3] Phoebe is cited as the first woman to bear the title in the early New Testament church, a forbearer of those deaconesses to follow her in subsequent centuries.

Deaconesses in the nineteenth century set out to fulfill the Wesleyan ideal of "perfecting" American society by seeking to correct the social ills that afflicted it. By succeeding in correcting American society, a template would be created for replicating this same work in countries around the world, thus establishing God's reign throughout the earth. In the words of Belle Horton, a deaconess educator, "we must 'save America for the world's sake.'"[4]

The foot soldiers in this religious effort were the city missionaries and the deaconesses. Lucy Jane Rider, a missionary society leader, had an extensive background that enabled her to play an instrumental role in the development of the latter group within the Methodist Episcopal Church.

Lucy attended public schools and the New Hampton Literary Institution in Fairfax, Vermont. After teaching for three years, one of which was at a North Carolina school for freed slaves, she enrolled at Oberlin (Ohio) College, the first college to award degrees to women. After graduating in 1872 she attended the Woman's Medical College of Pennsylvania (1873–1875) in order to minister side by side with her fiancé, a medical

2. Lee, "Evangelical Domesticity," 293–309.
3. Meyer, *Deaconesses*, 11.
4. Horton, *Burden of the City*, 41.

missionary. Unfortunately he died in 1875, and Lucy returned to the field of education. She served as principal of the Troy Conference Academy in 1876–1877, attended the Massachusetts Institute of Technology for a year, and then served as a professor of chemistry at McKendree College from 1879 to 1881. She also authored *The Fairy Land of Chemistry* and wrote children's songs.

Born on a farm, Lucy was raised by devout Christian parents. Her father was well known and respected for his Bible knowledge. At home his Bible teaching would include acting out the roles of biblical characters, and he would illustrate his lessons by drawing pictures in chalk on the kitchen floor. The focus of Lucy's mother was that her daughter would "receive a good education and become a useful member of society." When she was thirteen, one of her friends suddenly died, and Lucy determined that she would live in such a way that she too would be ready to die. She gave her heart to the Lord and became a devout Christian.

Lucy found expression for her faith through involvement with the Sunday school movement. As a teenager she followed her mother's example and spoke at her church's class meetings. Lucy then became the Sunday school teacher of a class of boys. As an adult, she wrote Bible lessons for various Sunday school papers and was a delegate to the Centennial Sunday School Jubilee held in London, England, in 1880. She left her teaching position in 1881 to serve as field secretary for the Illinois State Sunday School Association until 1884.

In the winter of 1884–1885, Lucy was hired as the Bible teacher at the Young Ladies' Seminary in Northfield, Massachusetts. During this time she began studying the re-emergent deaconess movement in Europe, and she began to envision the Bible school she would found to prepare women to serve as deaconesses. Her work to bring an educational institution of this kind into the Methodist Episcopal Church brought her into her first conflict with fundamentalists. For them, involvement in the church and regular attendance at Sunday school were sufficient training for women to engage in Christian service. Lucy, however, didn't just want to develop a school that specialized in preparing women as deaconesses. Because other denominations were adopting the ministry of deaconesses, she also desired to provide training that would standardize practices utilized by deaconesses in their care of the city's poor and sick.

In 1885 Lucy married Josiah Shelley Meyer. That same year she established the Chicago Training School (CTS), a training school for deaconesses. She developed a curriculum that both supported the spiritual development of students and equipped them for service in the inner city tenements. "So as she (Meyer) marked out the policy for the infant institution she had in mind not only a comprehensive study of the Bible but studies in hygiene, in citizenship, in social and family relations, in everything that could help or hinder in the establishment of the Kingdom of Heaven on earth."[5]

Dr. J. M. Thoburn, a Methodist Episcopal Church missionary and later bishop, was seeking to have his denomination officially recognize the office of deaconess. Part of his research included a visit to CTS. Of his visit Bishop Thoburn wrote, "when we reached Chicago we were invited to the training school of Mrs. Lucy Rider Meyer. Here we found a noble Christian worker with the same problem in mind, busy, not only in pondering the subject, but arranging to carry it into effect."[6]

Opening day of the Chicago Training School on October 20, 1885, was a humble affair. It consisted of a lecture by Dr. P. H. McGrew, and there were five persons in attendance—three students and Lucy and Josiah Meyer. The school was initially located in the Meyer's home at 19 Park Avenue, with a select number of the rooms designated for instruction.

Teachers at the school were unsalaried, and students had to pay their own way. Most of the furnishings for the school, including pianos and organs, were donated, and operating costs above income from students were met by timely contributions from supporters of the school. Josiah, who had training in bookkeeping, became the business manager of the school, and later also served as its superintendent.

A new building for the CTS was immediately part of the planning, and fundraising began immediately with the Nickel Fund. A thousand copies of a fundraising appeal for the new building were pasted into "cheap little books" and sent all over the country, which brought in $3,000 in its first year. When this amount grew to $5,000 a lot was purchased at the corner of Ohio Street and Dearborn, where the new campus in later years would be built.

In 1886 *The Message* (later the *Deaconess Advocate*), the school's paper, was launched, and Lucy served as its editor until 1914. The initial copy included reports of visits made by the deaconesses-in-training and

---

5. Horton, *High Adventure*, 117.
6. Golder, *History of the Deaconess Movement*, 314.

a typical weekly class schedule. Structured into the students' week were medical lectures, Bible lessons, visitation, singing practice, church history lectures, and assistance at industrial schools.

In the summer of 1887 the groundwork for a Deaconess home was begun, and CTS facilities were used until a separate building could be secured. The purpose of the home was "to receive such ladies as shall be approved, and for whom we can find suitable openings, who wish to devote their time to City Missionary Work."[7] Also in this year, Lucy received an MD degree from the Woman's Medical College of Chicago. This training would enable her to add a medical branch to her ministry.

Added to the Chicago Training School and the Chicago Deaconess Home would be the Wesley Memorial Hospital, the Deaconess Home for Old People of Edgewater, Illinois, and the Deaconess Orphanage in Lake Buff. Lucy was also to play a significant role in organizing the Bethany Deaconess Hospital of Kansas City. As each new facet of her ministry developed, Lucy enjoyed the support of official Methodist bodies such as the Chicago Methodist Episcopal Preacher's Meeting, the Woman's Foreign and Woman's Home Missionary Societies, the Rock River Annual Conference, and the General Conference of the Methodist Episcopal Church.

Fundamentalists, however, continued to fight Meyer's work in the deaconess movement on three fronts: 1) their original argument that the local church and Sunday school were the only training that women needed for Christian work; 2) objections regarding the deaconess uniform Meyer had designed, as it was viewed as a step backwards towards Roman Catholicism; and 3) opposition of Meyer's acceptance and teaching of biblical criticism at CTS.

Still, Lucy continued undaunted. By the time Lucy and Josiah resigned from the Chicago Training School in 1917 as principal and superintendent, "at least 5,000 women were consecrated into the deaconess order. She and her graduates have been credited with founding more than 40 major Methodist institutions, including hospitals, orphanages, and homes for the elderly."[8]

According to a Methodist Episcopal Church historian, that opening day of the CTS with three students present "will forever be a red-letter day

---

7. Meyer, *Deaconesses*, 148.
8. Prelinger and Keller, "Function of Female Bonding," 236.

in the history of American Methodism. From it dates the beginning of the Deaconess Work in the Methodist Episcopal Church of America."[9]

Lucy's achievements in the deaconess movement were such that late in her career she would be introduced as the "Archbishop of Deaconesses."

---

9. Golder, *History of the Deaconess Movement*, 315.

4

It All Began as a One-Room Schoolhouse

Fannie Suddarth

Directly linked to the history of the Methodist Church in the United States are the beginnings of a one-room schoolhouse for an elementary school established to "promote the holiness standards and doctrine,"[1] which would one day develop into a holiness college.

In the small town of Vilonia, located thirty-five miles north of Little Rock, Arkansas, Rev. J. H. Ferris, the pastor of the local Methodist church, experienced the "second blessing" of entire sanctification. This occurred at a camp meeting led by Dr. E. F. Walker, a holiness Presbyterian evangelist (and later a Nazarene general superintendent) in the nearby city of Beebe. Members of Ferris's church were also in attendance at the camp meeting, and with his encouragement about twenty-five of them also experienced this sanctification.

Upon their return to the church services in Vilonia, the pastor and these congregants began sharing their testimonies with the rest of the congregation. To their surprise, these testimonies were not well received. Pastor Ferris soon took another church appointment, and the resistance to the group that had experienced sanctification grew to the point that they were expelled from the Methodist Church.

Noah Simpson, a Vilonia merchant who was part of the group kicked out of the Methodist Church, was anxious that a Holiness work begin in his city. With the help of his fellow Holiness adherents, a tent was put up on the turnip patch he owned, where meetings were conducted by Rev.

---

1. Gresham and Gresham, *From Many Came One*, 35.

Bob Cook of Greenbrier, a noted evangelist. In 1899 a tabernacle for the Holiness congregation was built nearby.

This group then joined forces with members of the Free Methodist Church to form the Holiness Association. Ironically, this merger was most significant because the origins of both these groups included being expelled from the Methodist Church. The Free Methodist Church was established on August 23, 1860, under the leadership of Benjamin T. Roberts. A former teacher and lawyer, Roberts graduated from Wesleyan University when he answered his call to ministry. His advocacy for returning the Methodist Episcopal Church to the doctrines and practices of "primitive Methodism" led to the denomination expelling Roberts and those who shared his beliefs.

The Free Methodists had a three-fold belief based on the notion of freedom. The first was a strong anti-slavery stance, which was potentially volatile as this was the year before the Civil War began and the Free Methodists felt that the Methodist Church's response to slavery was lukewarm. The second tenet was that the seats in the church should be free, not rented or sold, as this practice promoted class distinctions and discriminated against the poor. Instead they believed that tithes and offerings should support the ministries of the church. Finally, the Free Methodists wanted to return the church to a "free" environment where the Holy Spirit reigned, as opposed to strict formality. Two distinctives of this new denomination were "being intentionally involved the lives of the socially dispossessed"[2] and its leader's strong advocacy for the ordination of women.

Roberts's advocacy for equal status of women in ministry was both practical, in terms of meeting the needs of the church, and based on his understanding of Scripture. Of the first aspect, he advised, "men had better busy themselves in building up the temple of God instead of employing their time in pushing from the scaffold their sisters, who are both able and willing to work with them side by side."[3] As to Scripture, he pointed out that "in the New Testament Church, woman and well as man, filled the office of Apostle, Prophet, Deacon or preacher, and Pastor. There is not the slightest evidence that the function of any of these offices, filled by a woman, were different from what they were when filled by a man. Woman

---

2. Callen, *Discerning the Divine God*, 146.
3. Stanley, *Holy Boldness*, 9.

took part in governing the Apostolic Church."[4] Although women were not ordained during his tenure in leadership of the denomination, the Free Methodists began ordaining women in 1907 and put women's ministerial ordination on par with men in 1974.

With the Holiness Association now formed between the Free Methodists and the local Vilonia congregation, Noah Simpson and Rev. W. F. Dallas formed a Board of Stockholders in January 1900. One of its first accomplishments was to open an elementary school, with Fannie E. Suddarth as its teacher and principal, who served at the school from 1900 to 1902.

In 1905 the high school and college curricula were added, and C. L. Hawkins, an Asbury College alumnus, was selected to serve as the school's first president. Originally the Holiness Academy, the school later changed its name to Arkansas Holiness College to reflect its expanded curricular profile. The Bible was the central source of knowledge and the school emphasized holiness and good scholarship. Worship was held in the dining commons each morning and evening, and the students conducted the daily noontime prayer meeting.

"It was under Free Methodist auspices until 1906, when J. D. Scott took charge [founder of the Arkansas Holiness Association] after a fire destroyed his school building at Old Cove. E. H. Sheeks, Joseph N. Speakes, and other members of the Arkansas Council were added to the board at this point. However, the actual operation of the college was for many years farmed out under contract to President C. L. Hawkins; it remained technically independent of denominational ties. Many pastors and evangelists later prominent in the Church of the Nazarene, including Lewis and D. Shelby Corlett and J. E. Moore Sr., received their initial training at Vilonia."[5]

The school "became an institution of the Eastern Council of the Holiness Church of Christ in 1906. After the Holiness Church of Christ merged with the Pentecostal Church of the Nazarene, the school at Vilonia functioned as an institution of the Arkansas District after 1908."[6] In 1914, the Arkansas Holiness College was recognized by the Nazarene General Board of Education as an "approved institution" of the denomination.

---

4. Stanley, "Promise Fulfilled," 146
5. Smith, *Called unto Holiness*, 172.
6. Ingersol. "Why These Schools?" 4.

In advancing the growth of the Nazarene Church in the state of Arkansas, Arkansas Holiness College played a crucial role in the denomination. According to Rev. E. C. DeJernett, "in the formative days of the Church of the Nazarene, the need for Christian education was viewed as paramount—with an uncompromising position taken by the Church relative to the credibility of the Bible, thus preparing workers to meet the needs of the growing church and society as a whole."[7]

The school struggled in the years following World War I, through the 1920s (enrollment in 1920 was over 200), and went through a number of one-year presidents. Finally, in 1931, the school merged with Bethany Nazarene College (now Southern Nazarene University) in Oklahoma.

While there does not exist much information about the life of Fannie Suddarth, she was raised in Harrodsburg in Mercer County, Kentucky. She joined her parents' Presbyterian church at the age of twelve after attending a revival service with her parents. In 1860 she joined the Episcopal Church as she was "attracted by its ritual and imposing forms of worship."[8] After she married and had her first child, she felt urged to baptize him. As there was no Episcopal church nearby, she joined the Methodist Episcopal Church South in Franklin, Kentucky, and had her child baptized there.

While serving at the Holiness Academy in Vilonia, Fannie attended her first class meeting. As she sat there, she kept hearing in her head her mother's admonition from Scripture, "Let your women keep silence in the Churches." However, as she heard the wonderfully joyful testimonies of her pupils and their parents, she lost her resistance to women speaking publicly in church and began seeking the experience of sanctification for herself. After three weeks of intense prayer and three days of "awful soul agony," she was "enabled to consecrate my redeemed powers to God and by faith received the Baptism of the Holy Spirit."[9]

After leaving the Holiness Academy in Vilonia, she began serving in 1903 as principal for the Holiness school founded by Mary Lee Cagle in Buffalo Gap, Texas. She was also secretary for the New Testament Churches of Christ Convention. It was during the summer of 1903, while helping to conduct the camping meeting in Rising Star, Texas, that she heard directly from the Lord, "you ought to preach." She later became an

---

7. "DeJernett," 3.
8. Hunter, *Women Preachers*, 91.
9. Ibid., 92.

ordained minister. Her prayer was that "God grant every woman called of Him may prove faithful unto death and that the worldwide Revival may find many precious souls brought to Christ through the ministry of women, who, with her brethren in ministry, shall by the grace of God hear their welcome from the lips of Him who had anointed them to preach the Everlasting Gospel."[10]

While her tenure was short, the impact of the school Fannie founded had lasting impact. Rev. James David Scott, a Arkansas Holiness College graduate and later president of the school, served as editor of the denominational newspaper and was elected as a Nazarene general superintendent. Lou Agnes White Diffee, a respected Nazarene pastor, evangelist, and radio speaker, finished high school and completed theological courses at the school. The Arkansas Holiness College faculty included J. Waskom Pickett, who taught Greek at AHC was a noted Methodist missionary and bishop in India.

---

10. Ibid., 93.

5

The Women of Azusa Pacific

PHILENA B. HADLEY, MARY A. HILL, M. ANNA DRAPER,
BERTHA THERESA PINKHAM, MATILDA W. ATKINSON,
AND ELIZABETH B. HARPER

DEPENDING ON THE HISTORY one reads, the founders of the Training School for Christian Workers were, alternatively, "a group of spiritual leaders from various denominations,"[1] "an interdenominational group,"[2] or "another [Quaker] group."[3] However, what is consistent across all three histories is that church leaders in southern California felt a great need for a school to train Christian workers . . . and . . . women were central to the founding of the school.

During the mid 1800s, the westward expansion in the United States included members of the Religious Society of Friends (known as "Friends" or "Quakers") who settled in southern California. By the late 1890s, there were enough Quakers in the area that they formed the California Yearly Meeting (now called the Pacific Yearly Meeting). In 1887, the Quakers established the town of Whittier, which was named after John Greenleaf Whittier, a noted Quaker poet. That same year Whittier Academy was founded, from which Whittier College developed. Chartered by the State of California in 1901, the emphasis at Whittier College was a liberal arts curriculum.

---

1. "Our History," 1.
2. Otto, *Azusa Pacific University*, 7.
3. Jackson and Murray. "Azusa Pacific University," 241.

Also of great interest to the Quakers and leaders of other denominations in southern California was establishing a school that would "prepare ministers and missionaries and . . . have a faculty and curriculum geared specifically to training these workers and sending them out speedily to their ministry."[4] Taking the leadership in this effort were Irvin H. Cammack, superintendent of missions of California Yearly Meeting; Philena Burdg Hadley, vice president of the Friends' Women's Missionary Society; and Levi Gregory, evangelistic superintendent of the California Yearly Meeting. They were joined by eight others, including Joseph H. Smith, a Methodist Episcopal evangelist; Allie Jordon, a Congregationalist; and six other Quaker leaders, in a series of three organizational meetings beginning March 3, 1899, at Philena's home.

Now organized, their second meeting on September 19 of the same year resulted in a constitution and bylaws for the school, securing facilities for the first year in Philena's home and recruiting of teachers. The constitution for the school set out its purpose as "not for pecuniary profit, but primarily, to provide thorough instruction in the Bible, and give practical training in all that pertains to HOME and FOREIGN MISSIONS: and to give such aid to such workers as may be practical."[5] At the third meeting on December 26, Mary A. Hill of Ohio was appointed as the first president of the school. She was selected for her extensive experience as a school teacher and evangelist in the Midwest.

Mary was born on December 5, 1858, to Joseph and Deborah Hill at Mt. Pleasant, Ohio. She attended Earlham College in Richmond, Indiana, and Mount Union College in Alliance, Ohio. She taught for three years at Friends' Academy in Iowa. While in college she experienced purification of her heart by the Holy Spirit. Mary was very active in the ministry of her church, and she had high interest in missionary work that was going on in China and India. Feeling a call to China as a missionary, she prepared herself by attending the Chicago Training School, where she also became a teacher. This was followed by home missions and evangelism work in the states of Ohio, Indiana, and Michigan.

In accepting the appointment as school president, Mary wrote, "it is especially desired to make this school a place of inspiration, as well as of education: a place of gendering spiritual enthusiasm; a place of implant-

---

4. Jackson and Murray. "Azusa Pacific University," 241.
5. Ibid., 242.

ing, and then of out-working holy fires. An undertaking in which God will search and work in the refining of hearts; awakening and strengthening holy purposes, Christ-like motives, purified, sanctified ambitions, zeal for God, love for souls."[6] With the motto of "God first," the Training School for Christian Workers opened its doors in March 1900 with two students, expanding to twelve by April. To assist with the personal development and spiritual formation of students, Elizabeth B. Harper (known as "Mother Harper" to students) was selected as the first matron of the school.

As additional students enrolled, Mary added new courses and more teachers, who generally served without pay. Meanwhile, Mary prepared the first school "Catalog and Prospectus," which paid tribute to both the Quaker influence and the interdenominational character of the school: "While the majority of those interested in this school are of one denomination, the teaching corps embraces persons from several churches, and these are selected because of merit and qualification, without regard to sect. All thoroughly evangelical Christians are welcome to its privileges. We wish to help fulfill Christ's prayer that they all may be one.'"[7] In addition to her administrative duties, which included recruiting twelve more teachers, Mary taught courses in biblical analysis, Ephesians, Pentateuch, poetical books, the life of Christ, and Hebrews.[8]

The Training School operated on the principle that instruction in "city missions was best obtained by practical work" and "instruction in church work was best obtained by experience."[9] Therefore, mission bands were formed with full responsibility for foreign missions work, and gospel teams provided churches with preachers, singers, and Sunday school workers. In the early years of the school, missions worked focused on China, Guatemala, and Alaska. The first of these missionary bands, operating under the leadership of Horace W. Houlding, left for China on October 15, 1901. Clark J. Buckley and Thomas J. Kelly pioneered the work in Guatemala and returned to the Training School to gather more workers. Unfortunately, before the Guatemala band arrived in 1904 both had died in Central America, but that did not deter the school's missionary efforts. The first Alaska band arrived in Nome, Alaska, on June 14, 1905.

6. Ibid.
7. Hill, Mary, "Interdenominational Character," 1.
8. Jackson and Murray, "Azusa Pacific University," 242.
9. Otto, *Azusa Pacific University*. 9.

The Women of Azusa Pacific

In the latter half of the Training School's first academic year, the campus was moved twice, first to the two-story house owned by Mr. Briggs and then to the Hotel Mt. Pleasant located at 1825 East First Street in Boyle Heights, California. At the end of the academic year Mary resigned as president to serve as a missionary in China. With the departure of Mary as chief administrator in 1901, the Training School would experience a succession of presidents (twelve in the school's first thirty years).

In reviewing her short tenure as Training School president, Mary wrote, "we bow in praise to God. Thus far we have come 'according to the good hand of our God upon us.' Ten different denominations have been represented in the ranks of teacher and student; which affiliation had proven a benediction to the school. Harmony has prevailed; souls have been saved; students and others, sanctified wholly by the baptism with the Holy Ghost and fire; life and service evincing the inwrought work of perfect cleansing and enduement with power at Pentecost."[10]

In the classroom, Mary's teaching and life had a great impact. Of the thirty students she taught, twenty-five became missionaries to foreign countries—five to Guatemala, one to India, one to the Philippines, one to Bolivia, two to Alaska, and fifteen to China. Mary's own departure from the TSCW was to serve as a missionary to China in the immediate aftermath of the Boxer Rebellion, in which members of China's Fists of Righteous Harmony (called "Boxers" by foreigners) massacred missionaries and Christian workers as part of their anti-imperialist rebellion. She made a brief return trip to the United States in 1902 in hopes of recruiting more missionaries specifically for China, and then returned to serve in this mission field until the late 1930s.

Once back in China, Mary joined with a band of sixteen missionaries in their work at the South Chihli Mission. She later spent a year ministering at the church mission in Nanking. In 1910, when the National Holiness Missionary Society was organized, Mary's application was accepted and she became a part of their work in Shantung. While her primary responsibility was working with Chinese youth, fellow missionaries appreciated her counsel and leadership. She was known for her consistent and powerful prayer life, and her dependence on the leading of the Holy Spirit in each aspect of her ministry.

---

10. Hill, "Interdenominational Character," 2.

M. Anna Draper, the second president at the Training School, served from 1901 until September 1, 1903. She resigned her position to serve at the Quaker Sunshine Mission in San Francisco. The school board then selected one of the Training School's most gifted teachers, twenty-six-year-old Bertha Theresa Pinkham, to serve as the school's third president. She served for just one year, until she married William Dixon. Interestingly, Bertha's father, William P. Pinkham, would serve as the school's fifth president, from 1909 to 1919.

Selected to serve as the Training School's fourth president, Matilda W. Atkinson brought a depth of Christian service to her work. Matilda came from Augusta, Maine, where she was the founder of the Water Street Gospel Mission and the Maine Children's Home Society. The latter ministry cared for destitute and homeless children. Matilda served for five years as president. She married Dr. Henry John Minthorn in 1917 and worked with her husband at the William Duncan Mission in Metlakahtla, Alaska. After his death in 1922, Matilda continued to minister to the Native Americans alone.

The leadership changes in the Training School's early years seemed to occur because these women were as much "doers" as leaders, both during and after their official tenure with the school. The home of Philena Hadley, which was used to launch the Training School, was also used to found a Mission and Industrial Home in 1909 to serve low-income Latino children in the Whittier area. Operating under the supervision of the Women's Foreign Mission Union, Carrie E. Wilmore served as teacher, and Philena as superintendent and matron. As a result of the school, the children "advanced rapidly on educational lines, but in deportment and in things divine as well."[11]

Each of these six women—Philena Hadley, Mary A. Hill, M. Anna Draper, Bertha Theresa Pinkham, Matilda W. Atkinson, and Elizabeth B. Harper—played key foundation roles in the school. "The strong influence of these founding mothers played a vital role in establishing the Training School for Christian Workers, as well as setting the groundwork for what would become Azusa Pacific University."[12]

---

11. Thomas, "Introduction" 1.
12. Otto, *Azusa Pacific University*, 7.

6

More than Deaconesses

Iva Vennard

On occasion, Iva May would recount an experience from her childhood that would significantly effect how she would journey through life as a woman. At four years old she was once not able to enjoy the entertainment provided by a traveling musician and his trained monkey because she and the other girls were crowded out by the boys in attendance. To make matters worse, her nine-year-old brother escorted her all the way home to her constant complaint of "Tisn't fair!"

She recounted this event to illustrate how deeply engrained it was that "she could never reconcile herself to a social code which put restrictions upon you only because you happened to be a girl instead of a boy."[1]

Iva was born December 17, 1871, near Normal, Indiana, the youngest child of Jacob and Susan Durham. At age five, her father died from the tuberculosis he had contracted during the Civil War. Her mother enlisted her entrepreneurial talents to help the family survive financially. Her business ventures included dressmaking, a hat shop, a photograph gallery, and a farm in South Dakota.

When Iva was twelve years old, Rev. Milton Haney, an itinerant evangelist known as "Father Haney," held children's meetings in Normal. At one of those meetings Iva was converted and soon joined the Methodist Church. At Christmas her mother gave Iva a Bible, which became one of her most treasured possessions. She became enamored with memorizing scriptures from her Bible, which she utilized as her "spiritual diary."

---

1. Bowie, *Alabaster and Spikenard*, 23.

When Iva was eighteen she attended the Holiness Camp Meeting held in Decatur, Illinois. It was one of the largest in the Midwest (10,000 on Sundays) and the preachers included William McDonald, Joseph H. Smith, J. A. Wood, and E. I. D. Pepper. Smith held revival services in Iva's home church, and in the course of these services she experienced sanctification. Her spiritual walk and pursuit of holiness was nurtured by her friendships with Holiness leaders such as Bishop William F. Oldman and D. J. Fowler.

Along with her religious commitment, Iva also focused on education. After graduating from the Illinois State Normal University in 1890, she taught for a year in an elementary school in El Paso, Illinois. While there her spiritual life faltered but that did not deter her from remaining active by teaching Sunday school and organizing the local chapter of the Woman's Christian Temperance Union. The following year she served as principal of a high school in Morris, Illinois.

Upon enrolling at Wellesley College in the fall of 1892, she came in contact with Dr. Charles De Garmo. He took special interest in her as a student because of her intellect and demeanor. After a year at Wellesley, Iva took a position as an English teacher in a high school in Tustin City, California. Her return to Normal the following summer brought her back in contact with De Garmo, who offered her a scholarship to attend Swarthmore College where he was the current president.

As she contemplated her future at Strathmore, a spiritual hunger was reawakened in her and she felt the Lord calling her to public ministry. Internal turmoil resulted, but ultimately she surrendered her will to the Lord. She then informed De Garmo that she was returning the scholarship he had given her. She informed him, "I've made my choice to be spiritual first, and that means my unswerving allegiance to Christ in every detail," to which he replied, "I would so much rather you would be a noble woman than a great scholar."[2]

Still, Iva's heart was not settled. After a time of prayer she reached for her Bible, and the Lord gave her the following word from Isaiah 60:1: "Arise, shine; for thy light is come, and the glory of the Lord is risen upon thee."

Now that she was determined to enter the ministry, Iva started a life habit that would endure until the last year of her life: asking the Lord

---

2. Ibid., 48.

for a "year verse." In that first year, the scripture was Galatians 6:14: "God forbid that I should glory save in the cross of our Lord Jesus Christ."

Iva preached her first sermon from Psalm 40:1–11, but struggled with the concept that she was really preaching. However, once started, she gave evangelism her full effort because she knew that her calling was truly from God. "First she conducted evangelistic meetings in area holiness churches, but following her 1898 appointment as Deaconess-at-Large for the Methodist Church, her ministry stretched from coast to coast."[3]

In her services, Iva sang using her mezzo-soprano singing range, played the organ, preached, and then conducted the altar call. For lodging she would normally stay with local Christian families. Beyond her preaching abilities, pastors also invited her to hold services because they were inexpensive, as the only financial requirement was that an offering be taken for deaconess work.

After several years as a deaconess evangelist, she envisioned starting a deaconess training school that would focus on evangelism. Although she initially encountered opposition, in 1901 she was informed by Bishop Fitzgerald of the Board of Bishops that she was authorized to open her school. After two years, the Epworth Evangelistic Institute was incorporated. Even though the school was officially endorsed and established, Iva continued to encounter resistance from the Methodist clergy and laity. "They objected to women teaching theology and Bible rather than clergymen and to women being trained in evangelism rather than religious education."[4]

In response, Iva was very clear in stating that the purpose for founding Epworth was to train deaconesses for evangelism. "Real, genuine, soul-saving work is the fundamental mission of all deaconess work, and no deaconess measures up to her privilege in service or fulfills her responsibility toward God who does not aim persistently at the definite regeneration of her people."[5]

Her dream of expanding deaconess work to include evangelism cost her dearly, both in terms of generating criticism and opposition to her plans, and in the future regarding her relationship with Tom Vennard, an architect who fell in love with Iva.

---

3. Harris, "Elect Lady," 17.
4. Pope-Levison, *Turn the Pulpit Loose*, 180.
5. Pope-Levison, "Iva Durham Vennard," 3.

To the man who was courting her, Iva made it clear that her deaconess work for the Lord came first, and any marriage would have to wait. When her ministry expanded to include Epworth, she indicated to Vennard that the school would not be stable for at least ten years. In response he wrote, "then I'll wait ten years." Fortunately, they only had to wait two years, and Tom was a great support to Iva's ministry. He was keen to support her efforts especially because he saw her work as making up for the call to ministry he didn't answer when he lived in England.

Within the Methodist Church, Epworth had both supporters and opponents. As for the opposition, in one meeting, "the District Superintendent, who was presiding, spoke, 'Don't you see, Mrs. Vennard, that your insistence upon theology and evangelism is a tacit criticism of our preachers? Why are you not willing to leave that to us?'"[6]

Regardless, the work continued, and Epworth sent out missionaries, children's workers, and home missionaries to minister to Native Americans. Nearly all of the school's graduates were involved in deaconess work. The March 1910 issue of *Inasmuch*, the school publication, indicated that 8,404 individuals had professed conversion or gained heart purity through the ministry of the school and its students and graduates.[7]

During 1909 there were crises in many aspects of Iva's life and ministry. She became very ill, and her husband had to take a job in Chicago as there was no work locally. Her family and school were both struggling financially. To cap these problems, the Board Extension of the Methodist Church demanded that Epworth's board of trustees convert the school into a Methodist hospital. Only the support of Bishop Fitzgerald helped Iva weather this latter challenge.

At this time the Methodist Church was experiencing the influence of modernism, and Vennard had to make a choice as the church was looking to change the character of the school she founded. While on maternity leave, "her opponents took matters into their own hands and revised the school charter, removed evangelism from the curriculum, and replaced Epworth's female faculty with clergymen. Iva resigned as Principal of Epworth Evangelistic Institute scarcely eight years after she founded the school."[8]

---

6. Bowie, *Alabaster and Spikenard*, 149.
7. Ibid., 158.
8. Pope-Levison, *Turn the Pulpit Loose*, 180–81.

Undeterred, the next fall in 1910 Iva opened the Chicago Evangelistic Institute, a coeducational Holiness training school open to students of differing denominations. In arguing the rationale of the school, Iva wrote "if the conception of the work of the holiness movement is sound, then the need of an interdenominational holiness training school is imperative for the equipment of young people to stand as leaders in all the churches for the pressing of this glorious warfare."[9]

Along with founding CEI, that same year Iva played a crucial role in the founding of the National Holiness Missionary Society. The leaders of the National Holiness Association were in the process of organizing a missionary society and asked Iva to help with the venture. She complied and wrote the constitution for the society and was elected its first secretary.

Iva also used her writing skills to further the work of the Holiness movement by publishing *Revelation* in 1914 and *Upper Room Messages* in 1916. She also served for thirty years as editor of *Heart and Life*, a monthly holiness publication. In 1915 she participated in the group that compiled and published *Heart and Life Songs*, a collection of Holiness music.

At both Epworth and CEI, women were trained to be evangelists, pastors, missionaries, and Christian workers. At CEI, equal opportunities were given to men and women to participate and excel in preaching and the school's radio ministry. Ironically it was usually the women who won the preaching awards. *Inasmuch* regularly carried news about women's issues worldwide.

Shortly after her death, CEI was relocated to rural Iowa from Chicago. During her lifetime, Iva had resisted this move because her heart was in urban ministry.

The school was renamed Vennard College in honor of its founder in 1959. Due to financial difficulties, the college closed briefly in the mid 1990s and was reopened in 1996. Unfortunately, Vennard College closed a second and final time on November 22, 2008.

---

9. Vennard, "Thou Are Come to the Kingdom," 6, 8.

7

Praying Together to Convince a Reluctant Founding President

Bible College Prayer Circle

There are individuals who envision a particular work of God, and those who, for various reasons, officially get the credit for its founding. Such was the case with Pacific Bible College of the Pentecostal Church of the Nazarene. "It is commonly asserted that Phineas Bresee was the college's founder, and in a larger sense that is true. But if being a founder means being the initiator, then [Phineas Franklin] Bresee is not its founder."[1]

The origin of Bible College Prayer Circle was based on three concerns of a small group of holiness people: 1) abandonment of the Wesleyan holiness doctrine by the Methodist church; 2) extremism within the Holiness movement in the form of teachings about the "third blessing" and "strange fire"; and 3) worry that since there was no local missionary training school, young people might end up attending colleges where their faith commitment and belief in holiness would be mocked. This group was composed of Martha L. Seymour, the wife of a prominent Los Angeles physician, Leora Maris and her mother, and Mr. and Mrs. Herbert Johnson. Ultimately, the Bible College Prayer Circle would be comprised of six women from three different Holiness churches.

They began praying in 1897 for the founding of a Bible college. It would be a five-year journey of consistent prayer until their request was fulfilled. Because the group wanted to establish the school under the

---

1. Ingersol, "Why These Schools?" 1.

auspices of the newly formed Nazarene Church, it was crucial to gain the support of Phineas Bresee, the founder and president of the growing denomination. Putting feet to their prayers, the six women joined Bresee's church and enlisted C. W. Ruth to represent them in their lobbying efforts with Bresee.

Although born in Franklin, New York, Breese's main ministry and leadership within the Methodist Church was in the state of Iowa. There he served as a pastor for twenty years, and the effectiveness of his ministry was recognized by his appointment as the presiding elder of an Iowa district. Breese was equally involved in education, and he served as a trustee at Cornell College, Western Iowa Collegiate Institute, Garrett Biblical Institute of Chicago, and the Indianola Male and Female Academy. He was instrumental in the upgrade of the latter academy into a four-year college, which became Simpson College, named for Methodist bishop Matthew Simpson.

Breese was twenty-two years old when Abraham Lincoln was elected president, and thus the Civil War was an important part of his life. An abolitionist and a Union man, Breese's beliefs came through in his sermons and on the pulpit, which he draped with American flags. Breese's preaching was revivalist in style and he believed that Christians should invest their energies in addressing the ills of society and the needs of those less fortunate. Years into his ministry, Breese had his own crisis of faith when he confronted his pride and doubts. His inner turmoil ended when one night, at the close of the service, he answered the altar he himself had just given. Kneeling in prayer, he thus experienced sanctification.

Unfortunately, his personal finances took a tumble through a mining stock speculation that left him broke. He vowed never again to enter into such wealth accumulation schemes, and feeling his reputation tarnished, he decided to relocate out of the state of Iowa. Through a thousand-dollar loan from a friend, Breese was able to finance a move to Los Angeles, California.

His ministry in southern California began upon being appointed pastor of the largest Methodist church in the area, the Los Angeles First Church. The congregation reflected the religious tension within Methodism at the time, with half of the congregation wanting a "fashionable" church and the other half wanting a Holiness church. In his preaching Breese sided with the latter half as his sermons focused on the Holiness experience. As he did in Iowa, Breese also involved himself in higher education. He served as a trustee at the University of Southern California and as board chair of the school's College of Liberal Arts. He was also appointed the presiding elder of the Los Angeles district of the Methodist Church.

A proponent of personal holiness, his efforts made him a target both in the community and within the Methodist Church. He championed the temperance cause and was burned in effigy by members of the local liquor interests. His stand for holiness ran counter to that held by the newly appointed Methodist bishop of Los Angeles, and Bresee was appointed to smaller and smaller churches.

Bresee believed that the best decision was to resign from the Methodist Church which he had served for thirty-seven years, and he began ministering to the poor in a skid row mission. This effort soon came to an end. Having run out of options, but still determined to serve the Lord, he started his own church. It began in a simple wooden structure called the "Glory Barn," and was named, at the suggestion of a friend, the Church of the Nazarene. Starting in October 25 with a charter membership of 85, the church grew to 350 within a year. Within eight years the church would begin to form a national denomination, the Pentecostal Church of the Nazarene, and sought mergers with other Holiness groups across the country.

When the members of the Bible College Prayer Circle presented their proposal to Bresee, he "consented rather grudgingly to the venture, but promised little or no assistance."[2] Breese's resistance seemed to derive from two sources: 1) he favored a school with a liberal arts curriculum, as developing this type of school was integral to his educational work both in Iowa and in California; and 2) having been involved with the development of a number of schools, taking on the creation of a new school may have seemed a bit overwhelming.

Undaunted in the face of Breese's reticence, Mrs. Seymour and Mrs. Johnson raised the seed money of $4,000 from their husbands. This enabled the group to begin the process of buying a large Victorian house and two smaller homes at 28th and San Pedro Streets. Herbert Johnson contributed $3,000 to the project, "asking only that the two upper-story rooms be reserved as living quarters for him and his wife, that no teaching contrary to the Wesleyan doctrine of sanctification should ever be

---

2. Smith, *Called unto Holiness*, 138.

allowed in the college, and that Bresee, Mrs. Seymour, Miss Leora Maris and Herbert Johnson be life members of the Board of Trustees."[3] The Los Angeles First Church of the Nazarene congregation raised the remaining $3,000 to complete payment for the project.

An organizational meeting was held at the Los Angeles First Church on July 28, 1902, and included Alice Baldwin, Phineas Bresee, Herbert Johnson, Walter Knott, Leora Maris, C. E. McKee, J. D. McIntyre, C. W. Ruth, and Martha Seymour. The group organized itself into the board of trustees, with Bresee as president. Although the original suggestion for the school's name was Bresee Bible College, Bresee did not want his name on the school. Instead, the school was named Pacific Bible College. The following day, the board was enlarged with the addition of close associates of the Prayer Circle, Dr. Seymour and Mrs. Lily Bothwell, and close associates of Breese, Rev. E. A. Girvin, attorney Leslie Gay, and DeLance Wallace. Rev. H. D. Brown, unaffiliated with either the Prayer Circle or Breese, was also asked to join the board.

The description of Pacific Bible College in one of its early catalogs gives a sense of the intended character of the school: "This college is not sectarian but is in the broad sense Christian, being under the control of the Church of the Nazarene. It seeks not sectarianism but Bible culture for all men and women who may desire to avail themselves of its advantages for preparation to do the work of the Lord in such fields, foreign or domestic, as He calls, under such auspices as shall be providential."[4] The school opened with a first-year class of forty-two students from seven states and ten different denominations.

Mary A. Hill, recently returned from missionary work in China after having served as the first president of the Training School for Christian Workers (now Azusa Pacific University), was named the first principal of Pacific Bible College. Recruiting locally, "she persuaded a group of the most pious and cultured members of the congregation to serve as a faculty and announced a half dozen courses for the fall."[5]

Mary's intention in returning to the United States from the mission field in China was to recruit more workers to help replace those martyred during the Boxer Rebellion. Her tenure at Pacific lasted almost a year be-

---

3. Kikermo, *For Zion's Sake*, 32.
4. Pacific Bible College, *Third Annual Catalog*, 4.
5. Smith, *Called unto Holiness*, 138.

fore she returned as a missionary to China. Mary was able to tap into the religious fervor at the school, and some of the brightest students in the first class at the school accompanied her as a part of a China band. Within the first couple years, three of these students died on the mission field. Mary stayed in China as a missionary until the late 1930s.

The true founders of the schools were dedicated members of the Bible College Prayer Circle. "The extent to which female piety and persistence made the school possible is plain from the list of faculty assignments for the second year. Leora Maris was principal, a post she held for many years. Bresee taught homiletics, scriptural theology, and Bible holiness one day a week. Mr. Seymour, who was a medical doctor, offered Old Testament, and Evangelist Joseph Jamison led the class in Old Testament history. The remaining members of the faculty were all women."[6] These included Mrs. A. T. Armour; Mrs. A. P. Baldwin; Mrs. Lilly Bothwell, who taught "Memory Drill" and "Philosophy of the Plan of Salvation"; Mrs. E. J. Kellog, who gave "Lectures from a Layman's Standpoint"; and Mrs. Leoti McKee. Mary A. Hill's legacy included serving as the founding chief academic officer (the titles were "president" and "principal" at the time) at not one, but two Christian colleges.

It wasn't until 1906, when Mr. and Mrs. Jackson Deets made a $30,000 contribution to build a new building for Pacific, that Bresee "joined enthusiastically in the plans to develop a 'Nazarene University,' comprising an academy, a college of liberal arts, and the Bible School, now renamed in honor of Deets."[7] The original intention of the Bible College Prayer Circle was to create an institution of higher education based on the Bible college model. However, under Breese's direction, within six years of the birth of Pacific Bible College, steps were taken to lay the foundation for transforming the school for training Christian workers into a Nazarene liberal arts college.[8]

---

6. Ibid.
7. Ibid., 139.
8. Ingersol, "Why These Schools?" 2.

8

You Will Minister in This Country

Mary Lee Cagle

RECOMMITTING HER HEART TO Jesus at the age of fifteen, Mary Lee Wasson set out to convert the fifteen members of her high school class to the Christian faith. This she accomplished over the course of the next academic year. Due to her success spiritually, Mary Lee was convinced that she was called to be a missionary.

When Mary informed her family of the call she felt upon her life, they reacted quite negatively, especially her mother, who proclaimed that she preferred a dead daughter to one who went off to serve in foreign missions. Her brother-in-law added that if Mary ever preached, his children would never be allowed to acknowledge her as their aunt. In response, Mary's fervor for answering her call diminished for a time. However, she continued her spiritual development through involvement in her church.

Mary was born on September 12, 1864, to John and Mary Wasson, farmers who lived near Moulton in Lancaster County, Alabama. Her father was a Cumberland Presbyterian and her mother a Methodist. Growing up during a time of northern Alabama revivalism, as a young child Mary felt called to "the Lord's work" and gave her heart to God. Her initial enthusiasm did not last, and it was not rekindled until she reached her teenage years.

Having recommitted her life, Mary's next step in her faith journey was an encounter with the Holiness doctrine. When Mary was twenty she attended the revivals of Robert Lee Harris, "the cowboy evangelist," and a member of the Texas Conference of the Free Methodist Church.

As Robert preached, "Holy Ghost conviction" and the "old call to preach" seized Mary's heart, and her "former joyful experience was restored" to her after three days of seeking to be sanctified.[1] While other women of her era found that the experience of sanctification helped them conquer the "man-fearing spirit," for Mary sanctification enabled her to embrace her calling "stronger than ever before."[2]

Now spiritually restored, Mary turned her attention to answering the call to preach. Although she felt a call to ministry, she thought it would be in foreign missions as opportunities for women in ministry were limited in the United States.[3] She also struggled with embracing her identity as a "woman preacher," both because she lacked role models and because the social climate in the South did not encourage her to do so.

To her surprise, God revealed to Mary that her ministry would be in her home country and not on a foreign field. This revelation caused her to experience turmoil of soul:

> On my face before God, with tears, I would plead to be released. I knew to go out in this country as a woman preacher would mean to face bitter opposition, prejudice, slanderous tongues, my name cast out as evil, my motives misconstrued and to be looked upon with suspicion.
>
> Besides this, I was so conscious of my inability. My educational advantages had been very limited. I was reared a timid, country girl and had never been out in the world—in fact until 27 years of age, had never been outside of my native county of Alabama. It seemed strange that God would call me when all these things are considered.[4]

At the age of 27 Mary married Robert Harris, and they immediately set out in itinerant ministry together. In addition to teaching Mary a theological framework for her Holiness beliefs, Robert influenced her future ministry in significant ways. First, she learned the art of evangelism by observing Robert preach. He too was a bit of a maverick, operating as an "independent" evangelist, though he was first sponsored by the Free Methodists and later by the Methodist Episcopal Church.

---

1. Pope-Levison, *Turn the Pulpit Loose*, 148.
2. Cagle, *Life and Work*, 21.
3. Laird, *Ordained Women in the Church of the Nazarene*, 104.
4. Hunter, "Mrs. Mary Lee Cagle," 71.

When Mary informed Robert about her call to preach, "he responded, 'I have known that for some time.'"[5] His affirmation served as deep inspiration for Mary. Robert also provided opportunities for Mary to develop her public ministry a step at a time, as she sang and led prayer meetings while he preached in their evangelistic meetings in Tennessee, Mississippi, Alabama, and Texas.

In 1893, the West Tennessee Conference of the Methodist Episcopal Church had had enough of independent evangelists like Robert and it passed a resolution calling the work of these evangelists, "in the main an evil of great magnitude."[6] The following year, Robert cut his ties with the Methodists and formed a Holiness church, the New Testament Church of Christ (which would later become a denomination), in Milan, Tennessee. He also wrote an organizational pamphlet for the church, entitled "The Government and Doctrines of the New Testament Church." This new work of God began with a congregation of fourteen devoted members.

During this time Robert was succumbing to tuberculosis, and he died a few months after the founding of the church. Ironically, it was as her husband lay on his deathbed that Mary fully submitted to her calling. She bartered with God, promising to answer the call if he would only heal her husband. God's response was, "Whether I heal your husband or not, will you do what I want you to do?"[7] Although she struggled internally, she finally submitted to God's will.

The survival of the church founded by Robert fell to three women: Mary Lee, Donie Mitchum, and Elliot J. Sheeks. The three women evangelized and organized new churches in Tennessee and Arkansas, visiting Holiness bands, conducting tent meetings in the summer, and holding services in halls and rented churches during the winter.

It was at a revival in Kentucky where Mary reluctantly agreed to be the featured speaker, and amazingly she was able to preach with "freedom and force"[8] and claim her identity as a woman preacher. She "turned the pulpit loose—she ran from one end of the large platform to the other and shouted and praised God, and preached with the Holy Ghost sent

---

5. Stanley, *Holy Boldness*, 104.
6. Smith, *Called unto Holiness*, 153.
7. Stanley, *Holy Boldness*, 103.
8. Laird, *Ordained Women in the Church of the Nazarene*, 109.

down from above."⁹ After a year of preaching she organized the first New Testament Church of Christ congregation in the immigrant community of Swedonia, in West Texas, an area that later would become her home and focus of ministry. Mary organized the first congregations in Texas near the city of Abilene in 1895.

In her evangelism Mary was noted for her initiative in going to preach where the poor and oppressed were. For instance, over the objections of her family she preached to African-American congregations. Wherever she could find a venue to preach—camp meetings, brush arbors, jails, church houses, in canyons—she would go. Impressed with the effectiveness of her ministry, one of the local newspaper editors referred to Mary as "the Mother of Holiness in West Texas." Four years later, in 1899, Mary and E. J. Sheeks were ordained during the first council of the newly formed denomination of the New Testament Church of Christ. At this point in her ministerial career, Mary established her permanent home in Buffalo Gap, Texas. Now a pastor, evangelist, and superintendent, she was responsible to guide a growing network of churches.

In 1900, with one thousand attendees as witnesses, Mary wed H. C. Cagle, a cowhand who was converted under her ministry and who had developed as a preacher under her tutelage. Mary's pastorate was in Buffalo Gap, which had one of the New Testament Church of Christ's largest churches, and she also promoted the annual camp meeting held in town.

Not everyone was in support of women preachers, or of Mary's ministry in particular. In Anson, Texas, rumors were circulated that Mary "had robbed the United States mail, run a house of ill-fame, and given away her four children."[10] There was no basis for any of these accusations; indeed, because Mary was childless, the third rumor was an impossibility. The minister who perpetuated the house of prostitution rumor only stopped when threatened with a libel lawsuit by a Methodist official.

As an administrator, Mary was instrumental in not one, but two denominational mergers. In the first, Mary served on the steering committee that drafted the guiding documents for the union of the New Testament Church of Christ and other Holiness groups, which led to the formation of the Holiness Church of Christ in 1905.

---

9. Cagle, *Life and Work*, 29.
10. Stanley, *Holy Boldness*, 121.

Although scant records exist about the nature of the institution, she also established a ministerial training school at Buffalo Gap as part of her work with the Holiness Church of Christ. Providing education for preachers and rescue workers was a central task of the Holiness Church of Christ. "By 1906, the denomination was supporting three Bible schools, located at Buffalo Gap, in west Texas; at Vilonia, Arkansas; and at Pilot Point. Mrs. Cagle's school at Buffalo Gap was always small, and ministered chiefly to the churches nearby. Mrs. Fannie Suddarth, formerly a social worker in Forth Worth, was principal for many years."[11]

The second denominational merger in which Cagle played a pivotal role was the founding the Church of the Nazarene.[12] In 1908 the Holiness Church of Christ and Pentecostal Church of the Nazarene united to form the new denomination. At the time of the union, 50 percent of the women clergy were developed in churches under Mary's oversight. Once formed, Mary continued her work of planting more churches. The following statistics from 1927 indicate the type of schedule Mary kept: 10,000 miles traveled by car, 13 revival meetings held, and 175 preaching occasions resulting in 216 conversions and 118 people experiencing sanctification. A newspaper article from 1947 about a revival at which Mary was the featured speaker credits her with "organizing more Nazarene churches than any other minister in that denomination."[13]

Like many of her contemporaries, Mary was an apologist for women preachers. On the occasions when she held two-week evangelistic meetings, Mary would always include a sermon entitled "Woman's Right to Preach." She used not just selected verses but the entire New Testament for the affirmation of the equal right of women to preach the gospel. "I am persuaded that what they were allowed to do when the New Testament was written will be alright now."[14]

Although she had been confined to her bed for two years, on her eighty-ninth birthday Mary Lee Cagle preached her last sermon in Rotan, Texas. Standing with the support of a friend on each side, Mary spoke for thirty minutes. The following year she went home to her reward on September 27, 1955.

11. Smith, *Called unto Holiness*, 172.
12. Stanley, "Wesleyan Holiness and Pentecostal Preachers," 19.
13. "To Close Revival."
14. Cagle, *Life and Work*, 160.

9

From Tuesday Meetings to a Bible College

Mattie Hoke

In October of 1895, eighty-two founding fathers and mothers, along with founder Phineas Bresee, united to form the Pentecostal Church of the Nazarene in Los Angeles, California. The denomination was formed at a time when many in the Holiness movement were looking for an organizational umbrella that would unite the various Holiness churches and associations into a national body.

Four years after the founding of the Church of the Nazarene, "one of Bresee's pastors declared in the *Nazarene Messenger* that the holiness movement in America had reached its zenith under the 'iron-clad government' of the popular churches; now, he wrote, 'something must be done to conserve the fruit of years of labor.'"[1]

What followed in the early 1900s was a strategy of absorption by the Pentecostal Church of the Nazarene—of Holiness churches, associations, denominations, schools and colleges. This strategy was followed not only as the denomination spread across the United States but was also followed in foreign missions.

At the age of nine, C. B. Jernigan received the Lord, and later experienced sanctification as a young man. On the day of his sanctification he felt called to preach, but unfortunately the congregations in his community did not want to hear his message of holiness. When Jernigan married, he and his wife, Johnny, became lay preachers. Again there was difficulty because the Methodist church didn't license women to preach.

---

1. Smith, *Called unto Holiness*, 123.

Undeterred, the couple formed a Holiness band with Rev. E. C. DeJernett and preached holiness across the United States. Often members of the Jernigan band preached to groups of women in their travels.

Jernigan organized the first Independent Holiness Church in 1901 and was its first pastor. This was the first church in the Holiness of Christ denomination that was soon to be formed. In 1906 Jernigan and fellow leaders of the denomination were contacted by the Pentecostal Church of the Nazarene and the Association of Pentecostal Churches regarding a possible merger of all three groups. In order for such a joining together to occur, Jernigan insisted that the merger was based on one doctrine. "Post and pre-millennialism will not mix. Tobacco chewers and clean men would not unite. We cannot afford to get tangled up with godless secret societies in a holiness church."[2]

After two years of negotiations the union occurred, with the Pentecostal Church of the Nazarene absorbing the other two groups. That same year, 1908, Jernigan was appointed the district superintendent of Kansas and Oklahoma for the Nazarene Church. In Hutchinson, Kansas, Jernigan established contact with the Apostolic Holiness Church, which was the result of the work of Mrs. Mattie Hoke, who used "Tuesday meetings" to lay the foundation for planting the church. Mattie Hoke was born on July 31, 1860, and was married to James S. Hoke in 1882. Two years later the couple moved to Hutchinson, where Mattie took a leadership role among the local Holiness people.

"Tuesday meetings" were foundational to the spiritual formation of adherents of the Holiness movement, since they were initiated by Sarah Langford and then continued by her sister Phoebe Palmer, the founder of the Holiness movement.[3] "This congregation was the fruit of a Tuesday holiness meeting which Mrs. Mattie Hoke began in 1898. A little band, chiefly women, met weekly for six years, sometimes in the homes of 'the very poor and lowly' and 'often with the sick and dying,' as Mrs. Hoke remembered it, and at other times, 'in the county jail, at the county poor farm, on the street, in the brothels, in the home of the banker and businessman, in the downtown office, in groves, in schoolhouses, in some of the churches, and in hotels and tents.' They stressed divine healing from

---

2. Ibid., 214.
3. Dieter, *Holiness Revival*, 22–23.

the beginning, and after extensive Bible study, adopted the premillennial view of the Second Coming."[4]

In October 1904, this band of women opened a Holiness mission that included a Sunday school and other regular services. The mission soon grew in number as there was an influx of Holiness believers into Hutchinson from the rural areas surrounding the city. A few months later, twenty charter members organized the church. The following year a large home was purchased for the establishment of the Apostolic Holiness Bible School, and the church was moved to a new location. The school began with thirty-five students, and with biblical scholar G. Arnold Hodgin as the main teacher and the church's pastor. That same year, the members of the church began holding an annual camp meeting nearby, which served both as an adjunct ministry of the school but also its main source of fundraising.

The purpose of the Apostolic Holiness Bible School was "The training of Christian Soldiers for the Battlefield in Home and Foreign Lands," and its motto was "All the Words of this Life, 'Till He Come.'"[5] According to Mattie, financial support for the school in its early years was strong. "The tokens of God's favor and guidance on behalf of the Hutchinson's Bible School from a business standpoint are many; and His leadings, in regard to selecting and securing the present location, are unmistakable. In the two years He has inclined His saints far and near to give about $7,000 for the purchase, enlarging and equipping of the property. And already many are praying and believing that the entire indebtedness of $3500 will soon be lifted. Psalm 37:5 has been most wonderfully verified over and over again, in the short history of this school, 'Commit thy way unto the Lord, trust also in Him and He shall bring it to pass.'"[6]

By the fall 1906 semester the school had a new forty-room building, which included a chapel for church services and a library. In 1910 an elementary school was added to the enterprise. With its location at 215 East 4th Avenue, the school was near the heart of Hutchinson's business district and public transportation, and "very convenient for street meet-

---

4. Smith, *Called unto Holiness*, 225.
5. *Second Annual Catalogue*, 1, 2.
6. Hoke, "Hitherto Hath the Lord Helped Us."

ings, house to house visitation, mission and all lines of outside work in connection with the School."[7]

Jernigan brought with him an increased involvement of the Nazarene Church with ministries established by the Apostolic Holiness Church. For the sustainability of these ministries, this involvement was timely. Given its location within a rural area, the school experienced difficulty maintaining financial support in subsequent years, and this led Mattie and fellow leaders to look to the Nazarene Church as a solution.

In keeping with the absorption strategy of the Nazarene denomination, the church, camp meeting, and Bible school were joined to the denomination in 1910. The school was renamed the Kansas Holiness Institute, and Mrs. Mattie Hoke continued as superintendent. The curriculum included courses in Bible, theology, English, mathematics, science, history, music, and German. During the early years of the school, students had to follow the twenty-one-item "Bible School Rules," a code of conduct drawn from both Bible quotations and literature, including "love is the fulfilling of the law" and "cleanliness is next to godliness."

During 1910, Mattie transferred her church membership and that of her family from the Methodist to the Nazarene Church. In the summer of 1916, after having served at the school for eleven years, she resigned, and Rev. Wilmot C. Stone was named president of the now renamed Kansas Holiness College and Bible School. In 1925, the school was renamed Bresee College in honor of the founder of the Nazarene denomination. In 1940 tough financial times led to Bresee College merging with Bethany-Peniel College in Bethany, Oklahoma, becoming the fifth and final college that merged into what would become Southern Nazarene University.

In addition to her educational efforts in establishing the college, Mattie's legacy included the alumni who served as missionaries: Peter Kiehn to China, Roger Winans to Peru, Viola Wilison to India, Eva Tixse to Africa, and Nettie Winans to Mexico. One interesting note is that the missionary group Peter Kiehn ministered within, which was an offshoot of the South Chihli Gospel Mission established by Mr. and Mrs. Horace Houlding, was absorbed by the Nazarene Church. Perhaps, however, Mattie's greatest achievement was being able to lead a process whereby a congregation faithful to the cornerstone of the Holiness movement, the "Tuesday meeting," established a Holiness college.

---

7. "Location," Catalog, 5.

In 1918, Mattie and her family moved from Hutchinson to Los Angeles, California, and she transferred her family's church membership to the First Church of the Nazarene of Los Angeles. She remained active in church work, teaching in the Berean Sunday School and serving as an active member of the Women's Foreign Missionary Society (founded by Susan Fitkin). On a personal level, Mrs. Hoke was "an earnest Christian in every sense of the word. She was a woman of deep piety and given to earnest prayer. Her interests were worldwide for she carried a burden for all of the mission fields."[8] She gave liberally of her own income to support the work of her church and foreign missions.

Mattie remained active in church work until her passing on February 17, 1938. A short illness preceded her death, and during this time she continually assured her family and friends that she was ready to go home to be with the Lord. Assisting her pastor, Dr. Henry B. Wallin, with the funeral was Dr. Roy L. Smith, pastor of the First Methodist Church of Los Angeles. His participation was especially fitting, as Mattie had been his Sunday Bible school teacher and had greatly influenced his decision to enter the ministry.

---

8. "Obituary Hoke," 158.

10

Mattie's Children, Mattie's School

Mattie Mallory

THE LATE 1890S USHERED in the birth of the "fire-baptized" Holiness movement. According to the teaching of this group, the infilling of the Holy Spirit was accompanied by a physical sensation of heat. This "third blessing" (following conversion and sanctification) was experienced by Benjamin Hardin Irwin, who explained that he was "at rest in a measureless ocean of pre-living fire. My fingertips were even hot and seemed to burn in the manifest presence of the in-working Deity."[1]

Irvin, an elder in the Wesleyan Methodist Church, would not only embrace "fire-baptism," but also join and become a leader of the movement. When the National Holiness Movement rejected this teaching, Irvin organized adherents of this new experience into the Fire Baptized Holiness Association of Southern Iowa in 1895. This move led the Wesleyan Methodists to disavow themselves from Irvin. When the association was reorganized into a denomination, the name was changed to the Fire-Baptized Holiness Church, with Irvin as its leader.

Adherents of the new denomination came from the Holiness associations in Iowa, Nebraska, and Kansas. This teaching of "fire baptism" would also have its impact the Pentecostal movement, which was born in the early 1900s. "Pentecostal fire" and "Holy Ghost and fire" would not only become key terms in hymns and sermons, but also optimal experiences for believers.

---

1. Irwin, "Central Idea," 4.

Mattie Maranda Mallory joined the Fire-Baptized movement and was soon identified for her leadership potential. In 1897, she was en route to a superintendency position at a Fire-Baptized mission in Winnipeg, Canada, but on the way she would discover that her leadership talents would be needed for a different type of Christian work. Her itinerary included a train stop in Oklahoma City. While there, Mattie must have walked the city streets and encountered homeless children, because she there received a call from God to minister to them.

Mattie was born 1865 in Ottawa, Kansas, an area of resettlement for Ottawa Native Americans from Ohio. Her mother and father, originally from Connecticut and North Carolina, were part of the "free-staters" and abolitionists who migrated to this area both before and during the Civil War. In 1889 she became the third person in her family to graduate from Baker University, a Methodist college. To her certification, Mattie added an additional year of normal training (professional training for elementary school teachers) at a teacher's college in Emporia, and two years of classroom teaching. In 1892, she was appointed principal of Dawes Academy, a school for the descendents of former slaves of the Chickasaw whom the tribe refused to integrate into their community. The school was located at Berwyn, near the city of Ardmore in Native territory.

Now in Oklahoma City, on that fateful trip toward Winnipeg, her sense of calling was fulfilled when Reuben R. Hershey asked her to establish a school for orphans and children of evangelists. It was to be part of the home and mission he had opened at a house he rented on Reno Street. Mattie immediately traveled to Berwyn and recruited former associates E. Frances Johnston and Laura B. Shaw to assist her with this worthwhile effort.

She started an orphanage in September of 1897, and by January of the next year twelve children were residing there. Mattie also edited *Guide*, the orphanage's official paper,[2] which began publication on September 16, 1897. The weekly consisted of eight pages with three columns per page, and an annual subscription cost fifty cents. It's motto was "No Law but Love, No Creed but Christ." Originally published by the Dawes Academy, after the move it was then published by the Oklahoma Orphanage.

The association with Hershey soon ended as Mattie and her associates felt that he was off-track spiritually. The orphanage's four workers and

---

2. Foreman, *Oklahoma Imprints*, 372.

sixteen children moved to a new location, with no money to cover the rent. They had with them "'only groceries' enough 'for one meal, dishes for four to eat from, and one little sewing table.' The women initiated their ministry on the faith principle, trusting that prayer, fasting and accurate information about the work would ensure adequate provision."[3] Three years later Hershey was charged with child abuse, which gave Mattie and her associates confirmation about their intuition of him.

The orphanage was incorporated in 1899 with the financial backing of the Fire-Baptized Church, and the signatories included Mattie, Wesleyan Methodist evangelist Estelle Gaines, G. M. Henson, ruling elder of the Fire-Baptized work in the Oklahoma Territory, and Benjamin Irvin. In 1900 Mattie's work with the orphanage suffered a tremendous setback. Irwin was arrested for public drunkenness and bad conduct in Kansas City, Missouri, and consequently resigned from his position as denominational leader. As a ripple effect the Fire-Baptized Holiness Association withdrew its support of the Oklahoma Orphanage. Undeterred, Mattie soon secured the sponsorship of the Holiness Association of Texas (1901–1903), the Holiness Union (1904), and the Holiness Association of Oklahoma and Indian Territory (1905–1909). Unfortunately, sponsorship did not necessarily translate into financial support for the operation of the orphanage.

In response to this situation, Mattie was able to use her entrepreneurial skills to ensure the longevity of the orphanage. In 1901 she used the proceeds from the sale of land in Kansas as down payment for twenty acres on the outskirts of Oklahoma City (currently the intersection of 27th Street and Classen Boulevard). Two years later, the orphanage was relocated there. In 1905 Mattie formed the Oklahoma and Indian Territory Rescue and Orphanage Commission to manage the orphanage and a home for unwed mothers. Two weeks after the commission was created, Mattie deeded to it eighty acres located one mile northwest of the site at 27th and Classen.

Mattie again relocated the orphanage to this new location and "founded the Beulah Height community, where a colony of holiness folk gathered around her enterprises."[4] Mattie "hoped that the settlement of holiness people around the orphanage would provide a model community

---

3. Jones, "Oklahoma Orphanage," 396.
4. Ingersol, "Mattie Mallory for the Children," 1.

and a base of support for the orphanage and the projected rescue home."[5] Six months later the new area officially became the Beulah Heights subdivision of Oklahoma City. Ultimately, nesting her orphanage and rescue work in a Holiness community would not work in Mattie's favor. The Holiness parents didn't necessarily want their children to associate or go to school with the "outcast" children with whom Mattie worked. This tension would ultimately cost her the support of parents and raise their resistance to Mattie serving as their children's teacher.

In October of 1906, Mattie founded the Beulah Heights College and Bible School, an interdenominational Holiness college "stressing purity of heart and purity of living."[6] The board of the school was led by Dr. G. W. Sawyer, a physician and former Methodist pastor. He soon stepped down so that Dr. D. F. Brooks, a Methodist pastor, Holiness evangelist, and Bible scholar, could take the helm of the school. According to the catalog for the school's second year,[7] faculty were hired to teach in the subject areas of Greek, Latin, New Testament, theology, mathematics, economics, history, English, and music.

In 1909 C. B. Jernigan arrived in the area as the first superintendent of the Oklahoma-Kansas District of the Pentecostal Church of the Nazarene, a newly formed Holiness denomination. He soon persuaded Mattie and her associates to join the Nazarenes. After having become acquainted with her, Jernigan identified Mattie as "a decisive force in establishing a 'safe work' (orthodox and void of fanaticism) in the state."[8] Mattie was a cofounder of the Holiness Association of Oklahoma and Indian Territory.

The campus property was sold, and the proceeds were used to purchase a site west of Oklahoma city where the city of Bethany was planted. The town began as a Holiness colony with the orphanage, college, a church, and a home for unwed mothers as the focal points of ministry. A Methodist minister, H. H. Miller, became president of the college, now renamed Oklahoma Holiness College.[9] The model that Mattie had devel-

---

5. Jones, "Oklahoma Orphanage," 398.
6. *Beulah Heights College and Bible School: Second Annual Catalogue*, 5.
7. Ibid.
8. Ingersol, "Mattie Mallory for the Children," 1.
9. Smith, *Called unto Holiness*, 227.

oped at Beulah Heights was replicated by Jernigan in developing the city of Bethany.

Mattie was concerned that the orphanage would be in competition for the church's dollars, and so she placed it under the control of the college. The wisdom of this move was confirmed when the Nazarene Home for Unwed Mothers closed seven years later. The orphanage she founded was under Mattie's direction until she turned over its administration to the civic women of the Children's Welfare League in 1920. The Peniel Orphanage, a spin-off of Mattie's ministry, was operated by the Church of the Nazarene's General Orphanage Board until 1929.

Beulah Heights College and Bible School founded by Mattie was renamed the Oklahoma Holiness College (OHC) prior to control being taken over by Jernigan. It is significant that Jernigan asked Mattie to vacate her seat on the board of trustees when he put the school under the supervision of his denomination. The main casualty in the organizing efforts of the Church of the Nazarene in the Oklahoma area led by Jernigan was Mattie's leadership role in the institutions she founded.

However, the central role of the school within the Holiness movement would remain intact. "No school in this district was fitting young preachers to preach a full gospel and, especially Sanctification as a definite second work of Divine Grace: and the question was, where were these to come from. The only solution of the problem seemed to be a school of the Pentecostal Church of the Nazarene where young men and women could be trained for the work of God and the church." The school has gone through four additional names changes since 1909, and today is Southern Nazarene University.

1912 was a very significant year in Mattie's life. It was the year she married R. W. Morgan, an aspiring preacher. In the November district assembly, Mattie responded to rumors that she had been expelled from the Nazarene Church by resigning from the ministry (consecrated deaconess) and her membership in the new denomination. For a short time afterward, Mattie and her husband ran a Holiness mission, and then Mattie was certified as a chiropractor and practiced in Oklahoma City. During this time period she joined the Methodist Church. On March 5, 1938, Mattie died of cancer and was buried at the Fairway Cemetery in Oklahoma City. On her tombstone was inscribed the word "Mother."

The legacy of Mattie's work with children continues today through the Children's Center at the Southern Nazarene University. In "providing medical care, comprehensive therapy and education to children with special health needs," the center's work is different from the original mission of the orphanage. However, "the primary focus on the well-being of children has always followed Mattie's basic principles based on faith, hope and love."[10] Because of a fateful train stop, and because she responded to God's call, "Mattie's children" receive the care they need, yesterday, today, and for generations to come.

---

10. The Children's Center, "Our Mission and History," 1.

11

So I'll Appoint Myself a Bishop

Alma White

When Mollie Alma White answered the call to ministry she didn't set out to become an enigma. Yet over the course of her life she alternated between behaviors that were iconoclastic and conformist.

As a feminist, she used the Bible to argue against traditional views of the "women's sphere" and argued for equality of women in the "public sphere," both in the pulpit and in society at large. In the area of religion, she was hypercritical of the Pentecostal movement, using disparaging terms such as "hallucination of Satanic powers" to describe what she believed to be the work of the devil.

Conversely, Alma's racial views and those regarding Catholic immigrants seemed to be in conformity to her times. She questioned whether Amanda Berry Smith, the noted African-American evangelist, should be part of a revival as it would raise the "race question." Regarding Rebecca Grant, another African-American evangelist, White commented that she was grateful Grant had "kept humble and in her place." Along with fellow Protestant Christians, White shared the anti-immigrant, anti-Catholic views of many fellow Protestants, and this led to a courtship with the Ku Klux Klan.

Yet this enigma of a person also founded at least twenty-five schools during her lifetime, including grammar schools, high schools, Bible colleges and a seminary.

Mollie Alma was born to William and Mary Ann Bridwell in Lewis County, Kentucky on June 16, 1862, and was one of their eleven children.

At the age of twelve Alma joined the Methodist Episcopal Church along with other members of the family. However, her spiritual hunger was not satisfied by church membership. Like many Protestants of the nineteenth century—Congregationalists, Presbyterians, Baptists, and Methodists—she sought the experience of conversion.

On November 8, 1878, at the age of sixteen, Alma experienced salvation through the preaching of Rev. William Godbey. He preached from Romans 6:23 and Alma responded to the altar call at the end of the sermon. "After seven years a penitent I had at last come to the end of the battle. The burden of sin had rolled away . . . It was as if I had been lifted out of hell into heaven."[1]

Once converted she felt called to be a preacher so she could share the gospel. Like many women in the late 1880s, she saw serving as a missionary as of the way to fulfill the call to preach, as there few opportunities in public ministry for women in the United States. Since the Methodist Episcopal Church did not recognize women's right to preach, this was especially significant for Alma.

Although she did not graduate, after attending Vanceburg Female Seminary and the Millersburg Female College, she earned teaching certificates and began teaching in a local school district.

Even though she was now teaching, Alma did not lose her desire to preach. During an annual conference of Methodist Episcopal Church in July 1885, she shared the testimony of her conversion. One of the ministers who heard her testimony offered her a teaching position in Utah, which she accepted. Because the Woman's Home Missionary Society underwrote her expenses at the school, this "was the closest she came to serving as a missionary."[2] However, due to the duress caused by the local pastor through his sarcastic remarks about her, she moved to Montana and took a teaching position there.

After a two-year courtship with Kent White, on December 21, 1887, Alma and Kent were married. Kent was studying for the ministry at the University of Denver and after the marriage she also enrolled there. However, the relationship between the two was rocky (and would continue to be throughout their marriage) and matters were made worse by Alma's meddlesome mother-in-law, who didn't want the marriage to work.

---

1. Alma White, *Story of My Life*, 1:223–24.
2. Stanley, *Feminist Pillar of Fire*, 15.

So I'll Appoint Myself a Bishop

In 1889 Kent was ordained a deacon by the Methodist Episcopal Church and was assigned churches in Colorado. Two years later he was ordained an elder. This same year their first child, Arthur Kent, was born on March 14, followed by Ray Bridwell Kent on August 24, 1892. During Ray's first Christmas he almost died of pneumonia, and Alma promised the Lord that she would answer the call to preach if God would heal her son. Ray did recover, and Alma spent the rest of her life making good on her promise to the Lord.

There was yet another important step in Alma's faith journey that needed to be completed before she had the confidence to enter public ministry—sanctification. Because of her shyness, she initially struggled with stepping into the pulpit. A seeking for the experience of sanctification that had begun in 1883 now became an obsession. Finally after a time of fasting and prayer, Alma was able to conquer the "man-fearing spirit" when she experienced sanctification on March 18, 1893.

Alma then developed an extensive preaching ministry, and between 1893 and 1900 she conducted more that three thousand revival services. "Coincident with an increase in Alma's popularity, prominent holiness leaders strengthened their opposition to women in ministry and refused to let her speak at their gatherings."[3]

As a result of conflict, the White family relocated to Denver where they set up a mission and held street and tent meetings. Having found no opportunity for public ministry in the Methodist Church, she created a separate sphere for the influence of her ministry and those of others. "Seventeen years before [1887], I was wrapped up in the old ecclesiastical mantle and ready to lay my life down in sacrifice on the altar of the Methodist Church; but she made no provision for me to preach the Gospel and therefore it was in the mind of God to establish a new, soul-saving institution where equal opportunities should be given to both men and women to enter the ministry."[4] It was in Denver that Alma founded the first of her schools for training workers for the ministry.

Against Kent's wishes, Alma formally organized the mission as a church—The Pentecostal Union Church—on December 29, 1901. "Two weeks after my return from the Coast, fifty persons were ready to cooperate with me and unite with the new church, the organization of which

---

3. Pope-Levison, *Turn the Pulpit Loose*, 136.
4. Stanley, *Holy Boldness*, 169.

was effected December 29, 1901. Two years later (1903) a four-and-a-half story building for a Bible school and church auditorium was erected at 1845 Champa Street, Denver."[5]

Not content to just win souls for the kingdom, she wanted them firmly established in holiness. To this end she established a community, complete with a Bible school, in Zarepthath, New Jersey. The work began in 1906 and by 1913 the community was well established. "At Zarepthath, residents lived, worked, worshipped, and ate vegetarian meals. There was also a school for every level of student, from elementary age through college."[6]

During this time the discord between Kent and Alma continued. Kent struggled with Alma's dominance in the Pillar of Fire (the new name of Alma's church), and he lost patience when after a series of services the local press gave him the designation "Mrs. Alma White's husband."[7] For her part, Alma had grown leery of Kent's involvement in the nascent Pentecostal movement.

Kent had experienced glossolalia (speaking in tongues, which in the Pentecostal experience accompanied the infilling of the Holy Spirit) and wanted Alma to add it to the beliefs of Pillar of Fire. Alma had met William Seymour, founder of the Pentecostal movement, when he stopped by Pentecostal Union Bible School in the spring of 1906 on his way to Los Angeles. In a gesture of hospitality unusual for those times, Alma invited Seymour, an African American, for dinner with her family, and asked him to say the prayer over the meal. However, her growing anti-Pentecostalism was evident when she later wrote of this meeting, "I felt serpents and other slimy creatures were creeping all around me."[8] She saw the Pentecostal experience as having its source in witchcraft and not as the fulfillment of prophesy and an outgrowth of the holiness experience.

A power struggle ensued in which Kent tried to wrest control of the Pillar of Fire and make it a Pentecostal denomination. Alma resisted and retained control of the denomination and its theological perspective. As a result, on August 11, 1909, Kent resigned from the Pillar of Fire and left Alma. He then went to his mother's home in Beverly, West Virginia.

---

5. Pope-Levison, *Turn the Pulpit Loose*, 137.
6. Ibid., 138.
7. Stanley, *Feminist Pillar of Fire*, 72.
8. Ibid., 74.

Even though she felt right in her protection of the Pillar of Fire, Alma was devastated. She considered Kent's resignation as her "Gethsemane" and later wrote, "I felt as if I were walking through the valley and the shadow of death."[9]

The church continued to grow, and to "mark her authority over the denomination, in 1918, at the age of fifty-six," she became one of the first female bishops in the United States. "The same minister who was present at her conversion, the Rev. William B. Godbey, did the consecration service."[10]

Although fiercely independent, in the 1920s Alma joined forces with a group of dubious distinction—the Ku Klux Klan. There were many reasons for her attraction to the group: a shared sense of patriotism; "an emphasis on law and order, morals, prohibition and opposition to modernism;" an anti-immigrant sentiment, especially strong because most of those immigrants were Catholic; and a concern about the level of influence Jews had in American society.

Conversely, Alma was a very vocal feminist at a time when the women's movement was waning. She used the pulpit and her publication, *Women's Chains*, to argue for greater freedom for women. Alma argued that the "women's sphere" was a sociological phenomenon created by man and not by God. Her sermons on this issue had titles such as "The Door of Opportunity Opening for Women" and "Inequality of the Sexes in Church and State."[11]

Alma was a committed suffragist and strongly supported the National Women's Party, which advocated for the Equal Rights Amendment. She also supported the NWA even though the organization used natural rights to argue for women's rights while she used a theological interpretation of the Bible. White's advocacy for women's rights both in the pulpit and society, and her strong personality, earned her the title "Cromwell in skirts."[12]

Alma White was indeed idiosyncratic, a Christian dynamo whose behaviors and views were both in keeping with and ahead of her times.

---

9. White, *Story of My Life*, 3:146.
10. Pope-Levison, *Turn the Pulpit Loose*, 138.
11. Stanley, *Holy Boldness*, 128.
12. Casey, "Bishop White," 14.

12

The General of the Kentucky Mountains

Lela McConnell

IN MUSING OVER THE difficulties of her early years, Lela McConnell answered her own questions about what a challenging beginning would mean for her life and ministry.

"Why did the Lord permit me to be born on a farm? Why did I have to work so hard? Why so poor? Why so few luxuries? Why did I have to rustle for an education? Why so much prevenient grace thrown around me from early childhood? To lay a foundation for a rugged ministry in the mountains of Eastern Kentucky."[1]

Born to Henry and Rebekah McConnell, Lela attributed her early spiritual sensitivity to her mother. While pregnant with the youngest of seven children, Rebekah would read the Bible, pray, sing hymns, and praise the Lord. This prenatal experience seemed to impact the life of young Lela.

At age nine, she received from God a call to preach and a vision that she would some day lead a group of Christian workers.[2] However, she did not come to know the Lord until the age of 13 when Miss Amy Plank, one of her teachers, asked her to go to the altar during a revival service in a Methodist church in Honey Brook, Pennsylvania. She then became a faithful attendant at her church's Tuesday night class, and found sustenance for her spiritual hunger.

---

1. Vandewarker, *The Mountain Shall Be Thine*, 11.
2. Ibid., 19.

In the area of education, Lela was mentored at home by her mother. A graduate of West Chester Normal School and a teacher for five years, Lela's mother instructed Lela in teaching and classroom management techniques. Upon graduating from high school, Lela utilized this knowledge as she taught in a Quaker community in Chester.

Lela later attended Keystone Normal School and then began teaching in Atlantic City, New Jersey. During her fourth year there the Lord called her to ministry, and she enrolled in the Chicago Evangelistic Institute (CEI), founded by Dr. Iva Vennard.[3] For this training she was especially grateful. She wrote, "I shall never cease to praise God for the years of training I received under Dr. Iva Vennard and her faithful faculty who helped me so much."[4]

Upon graduation from CEI, she was instrumental in the founding of a Bible college in Edmonton, Alberta. Health problems, however, led to her return to the United States. Upon recovery, she served as a pastor's assistant in the Central Methodist Church in Atlantic City, and in churches in Philadelphia and Bristol. As she was offered limited options for spreading the gospel, Lela resigned her position and began work as an evangelist. She held revivals where she both preached the gospel and promoted the experience of sanctification by leading Holiness meetings.

In the midst of her successful evangelistic ministry, Lela enrolled at Asbury College in Kentucky. She soon joined the Mountain Missionary Society, whose purpose was to take the gospel to the mountains of east Kentucky. During her first summer at Asbury she had originally planned to conduct five revivals, but cancelled them to answer a call to preach at the Free Methodist Mission in Breathitt County, Kentucky. As a result of her preaching in Kentucky, Lela found her life's work.

To accomplish her evangelistic work, Lela used contributions to buy a horse she named Beauty, along with a bridle and saddle. To provide musical accompaniment, a new Bilhorn portable organ had been donated. A trio thus emerged: Mary Vandiver was the organist, Irma Cook was the song leader, and Lela was the preacher. The horse carried the equipment and baggage as the evangelistic trio walked on foot to conduct revival services in schoolhouses throughout the mountain region of Kentucky.

---

3. Bowie, *Alabaster and Spikenard*, 180.
4. Vandewarker, *The Mountain Shall Be Thine*, 20.

However, Lela encountered much resistance to the Holiness message she so dearly embraced and shared from the pulpit. Local young men under the influence of "moonshine" would shoot their guns while sitting on the front steps of the church, and at times shot into the chapel during services. "I said one night in the service, 'Boys, there isn't one of your guns can pick me off. I am under divine appointment, and I am immortal until the Lord sees fit to take me home.'"[5]

At her graduation from Asbury College in 1924, the school's president, Henry Clay Morrison addressed Lela as the "general of the Kentucky mountains" in recognition for her pioneering ministry in the region.

How does one get the faith and courage to take the gospel on horseback into the Kentucky mountains, hold worship services while the locals shoot at the church building, and rebuild a school after it is washed out by a flash flood?

For Lela that faith and courage came at the point of her sanctification. "On July 4, 1904 God gave me my highest and best preparation for a pugilistic faith and militant leadership that day when He cleansed my heart from all the carnal traits such as pride, anger, strife, hatred and envyings, and the Holy Ghost came in to abide in His fullness... Someone has said, 'Holiness is religion made easy.' I have found it so."[6]

The year 1924 was a significant year for Lela for another important reason. Originally licensed as a local preacher in the Methodist Episcopal Church, in 1924 she was ordained a deacon, the first year that the Methodists began "ordaining women as local deacons and as local elders."[7] She later received her ordination as a local elder in 1926.

Her first vision was for a church, and especially a boarding high school, as her analysis of the demographics and educational opportunities in the area led her to conclude that quality education was desperately needed. Mr. and Mrs. J. G. Lawson donated twelve acres of land for the first church and school.[8] Dr. F. H. Larabee of Asbury College was in attendance at the dedicatory service for the campus and provided the name for the church and school: Mt. Carmel.

---

5. McConnell, *Rewarding Faith plus Works*, 24.
6. Ibid., 9.
7. Stanley, *Holy Boldness*, 107.
8. McConnell, *Pauline Ministry in the Kentucky Mountains*, 44.

"The first money given for the new church and school was $.50 from a dear little mountain girl. She had worked long and hard picking up coal that had fallen from the freight cars as they puffed up the mountain near her home."[9] It was from the sale of the coal she collected that she earned the fifty cents she donated to Lela's ministry.

Once the Mt. Carmel High School was established, Lela's vision expanded as she saw the need for a school to train Christian workers. The Kentucky Mountain Bible Institute was established under the auspices of the Kentucky Mountain Holiness Association in the 1930–31 academic year, and it offered a two-year course of study in Bible (later expanded to a three-year program). Two buildings that had originally housed a coal mining company constituted the original campus. The Institute started with two students and with Rev. Martha L. Archer as principal. Since Lela was born on a farm, it is significant that a farm was—and continues to be today—an integral part of the schools established by Lela in Kentucky.

Tragedy, however, would strike a few years later. "During the early morning hours of July 5, 1939 heavy thunderstorms caused a 20-foot wall of water to move down Frozen Creek. Since most of the residents were asleep, they were caught unaware, and over fifty people died."[10] Of the fifty-two persons who died, nine were asleep in the KMBI dormitories: three visitors, two students, professor Horace Paul Myers, and his three children.

Undeterred, Lela led the rebuilding efforts, and a new campus was completed. Since the area was undeveloped, building materials at times needed to be transported via horseback. Always equal to the task, Lela also participated in this activity. In recognition for her pioneering ministry in the mountains of east Kentucky, Asbury College conferred on Lela a Doctor of Humane Letters degree at its 1947 commencement.

As spreading the gospel was central to her work, Lela joined her female contemporaries in exploring the use of new media technologies. The thousand-watt radio station WMTC was added to the campus ministries in 1948, and Rev. Wilfred Fisher was asked to serve as station manager. The station broadcasted sixty-five hours a week, and the programming included preaching by Lela and other local and national preachers, news, educational programs, farm information, and music. It also reached out to

---

9. Vandewarker, *The Mountain Shall Be Thine*, 31.
10. Hill and Shuck, *Kentucky Weather*, 71.

the children from the local public schools, who would go on air to present what they were learning in the classroom.

The legacy of Lela, a person of such a humble beginning, continues through the educational institutions, churches, and ministry she established.

In addition to founding the Kentucky Mountain Holiness Association, "McConnell founded three other schools and numerous [mission] stations . . . the third [school] was the Kentucky Mountain Bible Institute, a Bible training school begun in 1930–1931 that offered a three-year religious program that prepared students for a life of ministerial service. By 1962 she had established twenty-nine churches and supervised 129 workers who pastored churches or were working in schools."[11]

On April 7, 1970, during the final three and a half hours of her life, Lela was surrounded by coworkers who prayed, sang, shared humorous anecdotes, and offered words of encouragement. Among her final words, she said, "This is a great scene—a lovely scene. God is going to send you money to keep this work going. I got that promised fulfilled. My end is come and my soul is full of glory. The gates are opening! I'm coming, Jesus!"[12]

Lela then went home to be with the Lord.

Today the Kentucky Mountain Bible College, living out the motto of "A Passion to Live and Teach the Message of Biblical Holiness," is fulfilling the promise given to Lela McConnell in the closing moments of a fully-lived life.

---

11. Stanley, *Holy Boldness*, 171.
12. Fisher, "Overflowing with Thankfulness," 1.

13

Now Is the Time to Open the School

RUTH KERR

ALEXANDER HEWITT KERR WAS born on September 4, 1862, to Scottish immigrant parents who could trace their ancestry to the kings of Norway. At age thirteen, he was converted during revival services held by Dwight L. Moody in Philadelphia.

As a wholesale grocer he helped establish the grocery firm of Wadhams and Kerr Brothers in Portland, Oregon. However, this venture struggled financially. In 1902, Alexander made a tithing vow,[1] committing 10 percent of his personal and company earnings to the church or to social work. Three months later he borrowed money to pay for a patent on a glass vacuum jar that could be sealed at home. A San Francisco glassworks company agreed to supply the materials, and the Hermetic Fruit Jar Company was formed in 1903. Within four years the business was profitable.

When the company's warehouse survived the San Francisco earthquake, this convinced Alexander that God was on his side. He also encouraged fellow businessmen to set aside a portion of their profits for benevolence work: "Incorporate yourself so that you will escape income tax. Tithe faithfully and cheerfully, and check on the fund for all good and worthy causes, expending it all for the up-building of God's kingdom, and trust God to bless you as he has promised." Alexander's commitment to the tithing principle—"every time Kerr makes a dollar, God gets a

---

1. "The Lord Helps Those," 1.

dime"[2]—in his personal and business life, as well as working to convince others to tithe, would be a consistent theme throughout his life. Raised a Presbyterian, he remained a lifelong member of the denomination.

In marriage Alexander was not as fortunate. In March of 1910 he and his first wife, Amanda, divorced when their two children were of adult age—twenty and eighteen. Six months later on September 30, at the age of forty-eight, Alexander was married again, this time to his stenographer Albertina Sechten, who was eighteen years his junior. Soon after the birth of their son, John Alexander, Albertina died after contracting typhoid fever. An active member of the St. James English Lutheran Church, Albertina vowed during their only Christmas together to fill their home with "the most destitute children that could be found in the city [Portland]."[3] The following year, Alexander fulfilled that promise, hosting a Christmas party at his home, assisted by his daughter and son-in-law and the sisters of his deceased wife. Fifty-six poor children from the "North End" of various ethnicities, and a number with physical disabilities, were able to experience the kind of Christmas the "other half" of society was regularly able to enjoy.

Alexander's third wife, Ruth Bertha Elizabeth Kalbus, was born in Bradley, Illinois, on January 5, 1894, to August and Doris Kalbus, immigrants from Germany. She was baptized at age three in the Methodist Church, and when her family moved to Chicago, Ruth received five years of catechetical instruction at Christ Evangelical Church. She was confirmed at age thirteen, and became a consistent tither at eighteen. Upon graduating from high school, Ruth was hired as Alexander's secretary at the now renamed Kerr Glass Manufacturing Company. One year later she married Alexander on February 21, 1913.

Portland was the site of the Lewis and Clark Centennial Exposition in 1905–1906. One result was a boost in population, as individuals ventured there because of the economic opportunities the event provided. In the aftermath of the economic boom brought on by the exposition, the city returned to normal. At the extremes, it was populated by those who had greatly prospered financially and those in poverty because their jobs no longer existed.

2. Ibid.
3. "Tots Feted as Wife Now Dead."

Now Is the Time to Open the School

William Gordon MacLaren, a graduate of the Moody Bible Institute and a licensed minister, responded to the needs of the downtrodden in Portland by opening the Blessed Hope Mission. At first, the primary ministry of the mission was to help newly released prisoners re-enter society as productive citizens. The outreach expanded to give women economic alternatives to prostitution and an escape from that lifestyle. This second effort led to the establishment of the Louise Home to provide temporary shelter to women transitioning back into society. As some of the women who entered the Louise Home were pregnant, providing a shelter for their newborn children became increasingly critical, especially as Portland was also experiencing a growth in the number of orphans in need of a home, and so the beginning of a children's nursery was added to the Louise Home.

As the services provided grew, so did the organization that MacLaren founded. Originally the Blessed Hope Mission, it was renamed the Portland Commons and finally the Pacific Coast Rescue and Protective Society (PCRPS). In 1913, Alexander donated the home he had shared with Albertina, his second wife, for use as a children's home. Three years later Ruth joined the PCRPS board of trustees, and her input and resources were invaluable. On June 11, 1921, the Albertina Kerr Nursery Home was formally opened at East 22nd Street and Columbia Highway with a great celebration featuring the children being served by the program. Ruth remained an active member of the board the rest of her life.

In 1915, the Kerr family moved to Sand Springs, Oklahoma, so that the corporate offices and the manufacturing plant would be in the same locale. Six children were born to Alexander and Ruth: Alexander Jr., William, Mac Rae, Albertina Ruth, Hugh Allen (who died in early childhood), and Constance. Ruth also raised John Alexander, the son born to Alexander and Albertina. In 1917 Alexander served as a "dollar a year" assistant to U.S. Secretary of Agriculture, David Houston. In 1921, after he came through severe illness, a second home was bought in Riverside and the family relocated there. Four years later Alexander contracted a cold while collecting Community Chest funds. The cold turned into pneumonia, and Alexander passed away on February 9, 1925.

Left with six children to raise, Ruth did not want to work for the Kerr company full time. However, she developed the advertising campaign, canning instruction book, and new recipes for the company. Over the next few years, a succession of company leaders passed away until company president A. Thomas W. Kerr, Alexander's son from his first marriage, died in 1930. Mrs. Kerr then became the president and chairman of the Kerr Glass Manufacturing Corporation, holding both positions for the rest of her life.

In serving in these roles, "she became one of the earliest woman chief executives of a major company. Since many of her approximately 1600 employees were women, she promoted women into some executive jobs."[4] As president, Ruth is responsible for the growth of the Kerr Company into one of the two largest canning supply businesses. Aware of new trends in the industry, she diversified the company interests by launching a plastic bottle manufacturing company in Santa Ana, California. In advertising, Ruth devised a campaign in which she utilized as display cases a fleet of forty Fords, driven by sales executives, which had giant Kerr replicas in the rumble seats. Her start as an industrial innovator began in 1915 by testing in her kitchen the two-piece self-sealing cap developed by Alexander, which revolutionized the home canning process.

Even though she had been a longtime active member at the Westlake Calvary Church, she experienced a moment of surrender to the Lord in 1933 following special services led by Walter McDonald. Upon returning home after the final meeting, she stayed knelt in prayer until "she knew He had accepted her as a life partner and a new peace broke into her life and heart."[5]

Ruth also followed through with her sense of responsibility to society. Previously, in 1922, she served as superintendent of a charitable institution for young girls with social diseases. In 1930 she sponsored the building of a hospital, a school, and the Ruth Home—now MacLaren Hall operated by Los Angeles County, which serves non-delinquent children. The Kerr Company awarded six scholarships annually to winners of the 4-H Club Food Preservation Contest. Ruth would also attend the 4-H Congress, held each year in Chicago, and would share her Christian testimony with the young people in attendance.

The vision for establishing a Bible training school was born in Kerr's heart in 1935. For two years there was no progress toward this goal, but on one night "in August of 1937 God awakened this Christian out of a sound sleep at night and the still small voice said, 'Now is the time to open the

---

4. Wilt, "Ruth Kalbus Kerr," 3.
5. "Program," 2.

school.'"⁶ As a confirmation to the message she had received from God, the following day Dr. John C. Page, Mrs. Anna L. Dennis, both nationally known Bible teachers, joined her in the effort to start the school.

"The Bible-Missionary Institute was incorporated October 29, 1937 by Rev. Leland B. Entreken, Mrs. Ruth Kerr and Dr. Elbert L. McCreery. Classes began September 20, 1937 using facilities provided by Entreken's First Fundamental Church located at 920 South Grandview in Los Angeles."⁷

Kerr's involvement in the school included contributing financially to the purchase of the Los Angeles campus, initiating and supporting the Women's Auxiliary, founding the Christian Service Council, supporting the athletic teams and music groups that represented the school as well as worthy students who needed financial assistance. During the early years of the school, Kerr's financial contribution to the school was substantial, totally up to 75 percent of the gift income.

After briefly operating as the Western Bible College, it was decided that the school would have a liberal arts curriculum and was renamed Westmont College. After some searching and much deliberation regarding a new location, the campus moved to its present location in Santa Barbara. Westmont is a testimony to a woman who followed the vision God gave her and contributed time, resources, and business acumen toward its success. As was concluded in the memorial program published at her passing, "To state that without Mrs. Kerr there would be no Westmont is not an overstatement."⁸

Having become an established church member, businesswoman, philanthropist, and college founder, Ruth engaged her evangelistic wings in the post-WWII years, spending summers with evangelistic teams in Western Europe. She also employed her linguistic skills interpreting the delivery of sermons in German-speaking countries. Whether in the United States or in Europe, prayer was an important part of Ruth's life. A "Day of Prayer" was a regular part of the Westmont calendar, and she would call together the Westmont family for prayer during times of crisis.

In the memorial program celebrating the life of Ruth Kerr, the editor-in-chief of *Horizon*, the student newspaper, wrote this tribute: "Mrs.

---

6. Wilt, "Westmont College," 2.
7. Ibid., 3.
8. "Program," 3.

Ruth Kerr—who felt the leading of God—held faithful to Him. To that same One we all offer our deeply felt gratitude for vision that was big and a heart that couldn't cease giving."[9]

---

9. Ibid., 5.

PART TWO

Pentecostal Women
Carrying the Torch Forward

14

Little General of the Faith Healing, Holiness, and Pentecostal Movements

Carrie Judd Montgomery

It was three o'clock in the afternoon, and two groups of people located a little over 400 miles apart were gathered in prayer. African-American faith healer Elizabeth Mix[1] had gathered friends together in her home in Wolcottville, Connecticut, for intercessory prayer. One state over in Buffalo, New York, the family of Carrie Judd gathered downstairs in their home praying for her healing from injury-related hyperesthesia.

During this simultaneous time of prayer, Carrie lay on her bed as her nurse Clara read from the Bible. After a while, "Carrie 'quietly and without excitement' declared, 'Clara, I will get up now.' For the first time in more than two years, Carrie turned over and raised up, then swung her feet over the side of the bed and began to walk to a chair."[2] Thus Carrie Judd was miraculously healed that afternoon on February 26, 1879.

Born twenty-one years earlier on April 8 to Orvan and Emily Judd, Carrie's parents were serious about their children's personal formation. Her family regularly attended church and also had worship times together at home. At age eleven Carrie was confirmed in the Episcopal Church by Bishop Arthur Cleveland Coxe. The early death of two siblings and the long-term illness of her father made her more reflective about eternity. Inspired by this, she devoted her energies to teaching in the Sunday

---

1. Opp, "Healing Hands," 238.
2. Storms, "Carrie Judd Montgomery," 274.

school, ministering to the poor, and working with the Woman's Christian Temperance Union.

Carrie's father also made sure that she developed intellectually as well as spiritually. "Seeing Carrie's keen intellect, he [Orvan] arranged for her to begin Latin studies at age nine and later French studies. Emily Sweetland Judd, who had composed and published some poetry before marriage, spotted Carrie's aptitude in writing and encouraged her."[3]

When Carrie was fifteen, she interrupted her schooling to accompany her ill brother during his stay at the Home on a Hillside, a sanitarium. While there, she assisted director Dr. James C. Johnson in editing *Health Magazine*, a publication produced by the home. Also that year, her mother introduced Carrie to David Grey, editor of the *Buffalo Courier*, who shortly thereafter published her first work, a poem entitled "Clouds."

Ironically, it was the publication of an article on Carrie's healing in another Buffalo paper, the *Buffalo Commercial Advertiser*, that brought her national and international attention. Carrie was inundated by letters and visits both from people seeking their own healing and from those who did not believe in the account of her miraculous healing.

The room in which Carrie was miraculously healed was set up by her family as a "faith sanctuary," and in 1882 she established the Faith Rest Cottage, a home where "the sick could receive comfort, encouragement, prayer and teaching."[4] Faith Rest Cottage was similar to other faith homes established in the late nineteenth century across the United States by members of the faith healing movement. Carrie also became involved in leading a network of faith homes in New York.

Carrie would make the most of the reinforcement of her writing skills in the publishing phase of her life. In addition to her autobiography, entitled *Under His Wings*, her other books included *The Prayer of Faith*, *Secrets of Victory*, *Heart Melody*, and *The Life of Praise*. The literary effort that benefited the Holiness and Pentecostal movements the most was her magazine *Triumphs of Faith*, which she founded in 1881 and edited for sixty-five years. It also served as a bridge between both movements, as it "provided a nonsectarian forum for a variety of denominations to express

---

3. Ibid., 272–73.
4. Warner, "Carrie Judd Montgomery," 905.

concern and teachings on common themes that greatly influenced the healing movement, social work and worldwide missions."[5]

Carrie's entry into public ministry occurred in the early 1880s when she began to share her testimony of healing. This was significant because at the time it was still a novel event for women to speak in public. Her ministry grew and in 1885 she was invited by W. E. Boardman to teach at the First International Conference on Healing and Holiness, held in London. Among her faith healing contemporaries, Carrie preached alongside Charles Cullis, Maria B. Woodworth-Etter, and Mrs. Michael Baxter of England.

Carrie found eager ears among adherents of the Holiness movement, and was soon speaking at conventions sponsored by A. B. Simpson in New York and other U.S. cities. An advocate of women in ministry, Simpson was eager to have Carrie preach at his conventions. In 1885, when the Christian and Missionary Alliance (CMA) organized, Carrie was a charter member and was selected as the recording secretary of the board. When asked by Simpson to join him in full-time ministry, Carrie responded that she felt that her work was with the faith homes in Buffalo. However, she and Simpson continued to share the platform as they spoke at Holiness conventions.

Carrie also associated with Holiness leaders such as hymnist and *Christian Herald* editor William Broadman, Salvation Army founders William and Catherine Booth, and Emma Whitmore, Dora Dudley, and Jennie Smith.

In 1889, Carrie experienced what happened when people crossed the race line in the South. Ministering with the Quakers to both "Whites" and "coloreds," she was quickly ostracized by churches opposed both to women preachers and to "'nigger preachers' (that is, those who preached among African Americans)."[6]

That same year, Carrie spoke at a Summer Convocation in Illinois, and received a fateful invitation from George Montgomery for she and Elizabeth Sisson, another convention speaker, to come to San Francisco to preach in meetings there. George was a twice-made wealthy man who made his fortune in the gold mines of Sonora, Mexico, and in the Pacific Stock Exchange. He came to the Lord in 1888 and was later healed mi-

---

5. Ibid.
6. Storms, "Carrie Judd Montgomery," 276.

raculously of diabetes and rheumatism. A romance soon blossomed, and the following year George and Carrie were married by CMA founder A. B. Simpson. One year later, their only child, Faith, was born.

The 1890s was a decade in which a number of ministries were launched by Carrie and George. In addition to being members of the CMA, the couple also joined the Salvation Army.

In 1893, the Montgomerys established the Home of Peace in a big three-story Victorian house in the Oakland hills, on acreage they originally named "Beulah." Home of Peace provided "respite for missionaries from more than one hundred mission boards. Within the home, she established Beulah Chapel [a CMA church] and served as pastor for its weekly worship services."[7] It also served as a port of departure and return for missionaries, a venue for raising financial support for missions, and a facility for transporting supplies to missionaries in foreign fields.

Carrie and George established a rescue home for "wayward girls" at the Oakland site and the People's Mission in San Francisco. Both of these ministries would eventually be turned over to the Salvation Army. Another parachurch ministry that they founded was a campground named Elim Grove, in Cazadera. Undenominational Union Camp Meetings were held there, and after Carrie's Pentecostal experience the meetings were called World-Wide Pentecostal Camp Meetings.

From 1894 to 1898, the Home of Peace housed the Shalom Training Center for missionaries, which Montgomery founded and which was administered by Mr. and Mrs. H. C. Wardell. The purpose of the school was to provide "biblical and theological training for persons preparing to be missionaries or Christian workers."[8]

The Beulah Orphanage was established in 1895 and consisted of three homes: Sunshine Home for older children, Bird's Nest for three- to seven-year-olds, and Rose Bud Home for infants. Once established, the Salvation Army took over operation of the orphanage in 1908.

Carrie received the Pentecostal experience in 1908 in the home of a friend in Cleveland, Ohio. That fall she used the October issue of *Triumphs of Faith* to invite others to travel to Beulah to partake in the Pentecostal experience. However, Carrie took a "moderate" approach to her Pentecostalism, and thus was able to also continue her fellowship and

---

7. Alexander, *Limited Liberty*, 24.
8. Storms, "Carrie Judd Montgomery," 280.

Little General of the Faith Healing, Holiness, and Pentecostal Movements

ministry with other non-Pentecostals. To the themes of holiness and divine healing, Carrie added "Pentecostal Power" to articles in her *Triumphs of Faith* publication.

Carrie and George embarked on a missionary trip in 1909 that included time in Japan, China, India, and England. The following year, Carrie established interdenominational divine healing meetings held every Monday in downtown Oakland. These meetings lasted for twenty-five years.

In 1914, Carrie became a founding member of the Assemblies of God (AG), formed after splitting with the Church of God in Christ for racial reasons.[9] She had been issued a certificate of "Ordination and Unity" as an evangelist and a missionary by the Church of God in Christ. The predominately African-American denomination issued ministerial credentials to many of the white Pentecostals who would form the AG. Carrie, along with Alice Luce, Sunshine Marshall, and Florence Murcutt, was among the first AG women to effectively witness to Latinos in the United States.[10]

George and Carrie had a significant impact on ministry to the Latino community of the Southwest. Their encouragement helped Conchita Morgan Howard[11] embrace her call to evangelism. Conchita ministered in Arizona and went on to be an influential leader in the Asambleas de Dios (Assemblies of God) both in the United States and in Mexico.

After first receiving a gospel tract from George in San Francisco, Francisco Olazabal visited the Montgomerys' home and there gave his heart to the Lord. Olazabal first affiliated with the AG and went on to found his own denomination, the Latin American Council of Christian Churches.[12] After his conversion, Juan L. Lugo was tutored in the Scriptures by George and Carrie. Lugo then traveled to Puerto Rico where he evangelized and established the Iglesia De Dios Pentecostal de Puerto Rico.[13]

Known for her interdenominational and ecumenical approach in ministry, Carrie served as a bridge between Holiness and Pentecostal groups. She also continued her ministry to Christians from the Episcopal,

---

9. Alexander, *Limited Liberty*, 24.
10. Espinosa, "Third Class Soldiers," 99.
11. Ibid., 102.
12. DeLeon, *Silent Pentecostals*, 24.
13. Ibid., 33.

Congregational, Methodist, and Dutch Reformed traditions. By virtue of her lifespan, she was also a live link between the original members of the healing movement and individuals such as Oral Roberts and William Branham, who would become leaders of the post-WWII faith healing movement.

It is indeed noteworthy for a person to have made an impact on even one religious movement, but Carrie Judd Montgomery has the distinction of significantly impacting the development and the theology of three—thus earning the title "Little General"[14] of the faith healing, Holiness, and Pentecostal movements.

---

14. The nickname given her by her husband George. Storms, "Carrie Judd Montgomery," 287.

15

Providing "Educational Fitness" to Those Called of God

Elizabeth V. Baker

Traditionally, Pentecostals have been suspicious of institutions of higher education. On the one hand there is fear that the church's young people will be lost to the faith as a result of attending college. Additionally, existing institutions of higher education, even religious ones founded by mainline denominations, were not always seen as appropriate places to equip its clergy. In the latter situation, the perception of Pentecostals was that the mind had been given precedence over the Spirit in the preparation of ministers. Although they claimed not to be anti-intellectual, Pentecostals opposed "an education that destroyed faith or reduced dependence on the Holy Spirit."[1]

Another element in this tension between Pentecostals and higher education was Pentacostals' dependence on experiential confirmation of one's calling and efficacy of one's ministerial effort. The educational background ministers brought with them to the pulpit took a back seat to the "anointing" in preaching, healings, and the manifestations of "signs and wonders." Still, Pentecostals founded Bible institutes, as had their Holiness predecessors, and in developing the curriculum for these schools Pentecostals "committed themselves to the centuries-old tradition that the Bible is a special book a revelation of God's will for mankind. Holding its teaching as normative and essential, they established their educational institutions with biblical studies as the integrating principle of the

---

1. L. F. Wilson, "Bible Institutes," 373.

curriculum."[2] While researchers have identified the founding of the Nyack Missionary College (1882) in New York and Moody Bible Institute (1889) in Chicago as the beginning of the Bible institute/college movement,[3] the Garrett Biblical Institute of Evanston, Illinois, founded in 1855 by Eliza Garrett, predates those two schools by almost thirty years.

An early example of a Pentecostal Bible "institute" was the Rochester Bible Training School in Rochester, New York, founded by Elizabeth V. Baker and her four sisters. Its two-year program was "strictly Biblical as we have the Bible as our chief text-book."[4] The curriculum included "theology, or the great doctrines of the Bible, Synthesis, or analysis of the Bible by books; Personal Work, or how to use the Bible for seekers; Ancient and Modern History, Church History, Homiletics, Exegesis, Dispensational Truth, Rhetoric and Greek, if so desired."[5]

The journey to establish the school began many years earlier in the lives of Elizabeth and her sisters. Their father was James Duncan, a Free Methodist pastor, and as a result, Elizabeth grew up to be "a Methodist woman of holiness persuasions."[6] Heartbreak, however, would soon be part of her life. Before she was twenty she and her husband were divorced because of his abusive behavior towards her. The divorce was significant because at this time in American history marriage was governed by the influence of Blackstone's Law. According to Blackstone, "by marriage, the husband and wife are one person in law: that is, the very being or legal existence of the woman is suspended during the marriage, or at least is incorporated and consolidated into that of her husband; under whose wing, protection, and cover, she performs every thing."[7]

In essence, when a woman married, she lost all right to conduct business, own property and enter into contracts. This situation, in the words of New York Supreme Court Justice Elisha Powell Hurlbut, constituted "civil death."[8] Because a woman had "disappeared" into her husband, these rights could only be hers if she had remained single in the first place, or

---

2. Moncher, "Bible College," 106.
3. Ibid., 85.
4. Wilson, "Bible Institutes," 375.
5. Blumhofer, *Restoring the Faith*, 78.
6. Robert, *American Women in Mission*, 249.
7. Blackstone, *Commentaries*, 442.
8. McMillen, *Seneca Falls*, 78.

her husband died or a divorce took place. During this era in American history, a woman's economic fate was the result of her husband's financial success or failure in life.

Some time after her divorce, Elizabeth attended a lecture of the Ohio Women's Crusade, an early version of the Woman's Christian Temperance Union. Elizabeth had little interest in the lecture until the speaker told of women who entered saloons to protest the sale of alcohol and then kneeled on the sidewalks outside these establishments to pray. Her heart was stirred and she had an encounter with Christ.

Elizabeth remarried, and in 1881 her health was threatened by a severe throat condition. Her second husband was a medical doctor, and although he called in specialists, Elizabeth's condition only worsened. Divine intervention took place when C. W. Winchester, the pastor of the local Asbury Methodist Episcopal Church, anointed her with oil and prayed for her. She was immediately healed. Elizabeth's second marriage was also not destined to last; she and her husband later divorced, in part because she embraced the doctrine of divine healing and because of her ministry involvement.

Elizabeth relocated to Chicago and became involved in Christian Higher Life meetings. In 1895, she felt led to return to Rochester, and she was rejoined with her sisters, Mary E. Work, Nellie A. Fell, Susan A. Duncan, and Harriet "Hattie" M. Duncan. Together they rented a mission on Main Street and began conducting nightly evangelistic services. The mission was operated on the "faith principle"—trusting that God would provide for the financial needs of the ministry.

The second faith venture Elizabeth and her sisters embarked on was the Elim Faith Home. In Hattie's words, "soon the Spirit began to press us to open a Home where those seeking healing of the body could come and learn the way to trust, and be surrounded with an atmosphere of faith, where tired missionaries and Christian workers could for a time find rest for body and soul."[9] In all her undertakings Elizabeth had a foundation for her spiritual walk in the writings of George Muller and in the premillennial teachings of Adoriram J. Gordon.

The beginnings of the Elim Home gave evidence to the guiding faith principle being slow in yielding tangible results. Prayer and periodic fasting for six months failed to yield rent money, and there were also fuel

---

9. Blumhofer, "Life on the Faith Lines," 12.

shortages. Like others in the 1890s engaged in living by faith, "the sisters reinterpreted difficulties as tests of faith. Every detail had spiritual significance as they participated in the cosmic struggle of God with Satan."[10] Their steadfastness, however, was rewarded, as within in a year the sisters were able to purchase buildings of sufficient size for the faith home and eventually a small publishing operation and a school.

When they moved into the new facilities, the sisters surrendered their privacy as communal meals became the norm, and they never ate as a family again. The "laid-down life" became the ideal, with individuals not seeking their own comforts but that of others. Resources were shared equally among all the residents of the home. The daily schedule included morning Bible studies, prayer and counseling with individual guests, and nightly mission services.

The scope of Elizabeth's ministry expanded in 1898 when she traveled to India on a missions trip, leaving the home in the care of her sister Susan. While she was in India, Elizabeth met Pandita Ramabai, the founder and director of the Mukti Mission. This mission was originally established in Bombay to provide shelter and education to child widows. By the time of Elizabeth's visit, Pandita had moved the mission to a farm in Kedgaon. At this new location Pandita answered God's call to utilize the mission to rescue and evangelize women and children left destitute by famine. Elizabeth's experience in India served to expand her missionary vision and that of her sisters. One result was in the area of fundraising: by 1915 the participants in the ministries established by the sisters in Rochester had raised $75,000 for missions—a significant amount for that time.

"In 1902 the sisters began to publish *Trust*, a periodical edited by Susan A. Duncan and devoted to teaching the doctrines of salvation, faith healing, the Holy Spirit, premillenialism and world evangelism."[11] In the tradition of other Holiness women, this periodical was used to raise funds for missionaries. Utilizing this print medium to provide financial support for ministry became a model for Pentecostal faith missionaries.[12] "Several years later the Elim Tabernacle was constructed, and in 1906 the Rochester Bible School opened 'for the training of those who felt His call

---

10. Ibid.
11. McGee, "Elizabeth V. Baker," 351.
12. Robert, *American Women in Mission*, 250.

to some special work but lacked the educational fitness.'"[13] The school opened with twenty students—fourteen regular and six part-time—and a faculty of five. Students without financial resources were admitted to the school with the assumption that praying for their needs would be part of their educational experience.

Elizabeth and her sisters seemed to be in tune with the works of the Lord around the globe. First they received news of the Welsh Revival of 1904–5, in which great numbers of people had their hearts turned toward God and holy living. Then they received word of the Azusa Street Revival beginning 1906, in which there was Pentecostal baptism with an initial evidence of speaking in tongues. Skeptical at first about the Pentecostal revival, the sisters gave themselves to prayer and Bible study for a year before concluding that the Pentecostal baptism was a valid experience. They also concluded "that God was responsible for the movement but not for everything that was in it."[14] For the sisters, Pentecostal baptism was more about empowering and aligning the church to its original purpose than it was about restoring a heavenly language.

At their 1907 summer convention there was a Pentecostal revival, and many in attendance experienced Spirit baptism. It was not long before Elim, with its church, faith healing, publications, and educational ministries, became a center of Pentecostalism. Ministering in the nexus of Pentecostalism on the East Coast, the sisters were also aware of those who questioned and criticized the legitimacy of women preachers. In response to this criticism, Elizabeth justified her ministry because it was a direct calling from the Holy Spirit. However, when it came to selecting a pastor for Elim Tabernacle, the sisters sought out male candidates to serve in this position. When no suitable candidate could be found, Baker and her sisters continued in leadership. However, they never sought ordination because they were women.

Elizabeth continued to lead the Elim Faith Home until her death in January 1915, and leadership of the ministries was continued by two of her sisters, Susan and Harriet. A few years later, Susan became dissatisfied with the direction of Pentecostalism and closed the faith home and school. Elim Tabernacle continued to thrive however. Although the Rochester Bible Training School was closed, the legacy of the faith lives of

---

13. McGee, "Elizabeth V. Baker," 351–52.
14. Blumhofer, *Restoring the Faith*, 78.

Elizabeth and her sisters continued through its alumni. By 1916, seventeen graduates had served as foreign missionaries, and the school trained a number of Pentecostal leaders including Afred Blakeney, John H. Burgess, Marguerite Flint, Ralph Riggs, Ivan Q. Spencer, Charles W. H. Scott, Grace Walther, and Anna Ziese.

16

Following in the Footsteps of Great Grandma and Mom

Virginia E. Moss

THE LIFE OF VIRGINIA E. Moss is reminiscent of the words of the Apostle Paul in 2 Timothy 1:5: "I have been reminded of your sincere faith, which first lived in your grandmother Lois and in your mother Eunice and, I am persuaded, now lives in you also." Virginia's great grandmother was a country preacher,[1] and her mother was active in the Woman's Christian Temperance Union crusades of the mid-1870s.

As a pre-born child, Virginia accompanied her mother as she participated in Woman's Temperance crusade work, which she continued to do until two weeks before Virginia was born, on April 3, 1875. The family of six—father, mother, and four daughters—was residing in Susquehanna, Pennsylvania at the time. Although in appearance she was a healthy baby, her nervous system was diagnosed as having been damaged. This caused great anguish to her mother who was concerned that her ministry involvement had been at the expense of her daughter's health. At the age of three, one of Virginia's playmates suddenly died. This tragedy led Virginia to ask about her own chances of survival and she was told by her mother that the doctors didn't expect her to live very long. Shaken, she begged her mother "not to put me in the cold ground as they did my playmate."[2] Her mother kept repeating the salvation story to Virginia, and this young child

---

1. McGee, "Virginia E. Moss," 909.
2. Moss, *Following the Shepherd*, 6.

experienced both salvation of soul and healing in her body. Unfortunately, her body continued to be frail.

In their home, Virginia's mother reserved a special "Bethel Room" for prayer and fasting. The two main burdens upon her heart during extended times of prayer were the conversion of her unsaved husband and "the lost souls of dark, sad India." As a child, Virginia would listen to the prayers of her mother by lying on floor facedown and putting her ear to the crack at the bottom of the door. One day she walked into the prayer room, where her mother was prostrate in prayer, and asked her what she was praying about. In response, Virginia was told about her uncle Dr. Clarenden Muzzy, one of the first missionaries to India, who began his work as a medical missionary in Calcutta.

She also heard about her mother's lifelong desire to serve the Lord as a missionary. As a young child Virginia's mother had heard the call of God to serve Him in India. While in college she had felt the call reaffirmed, and attended a Presbyterian seminary in order to serve in India as a missionary under the auspices of a Presbyterian board. With her education complete, her spiritual anointing for service came in the form of Spirit baptism at an interdenominational service held in a school house. She then traveled by steamer to New York, about to embark on this adventure of Christian service, when she received a telegram that her mother was very ill. She got off the ship and came home to take care of Virginia's grandmother. During this time she married, and with the exchange of the wedding bells came a "closing of India's call." Virginia's mother later left the Presbyterian Church and became a Methodist.

Her missionary aspiration dashed, Virginia's mother took comfort in the fact that her husband became one of "Jesus' friends," those individuals who may or may not be saved but yet provided provision and support for Jesus' ministry. Her husband admired people who lived sacrificial lives and enjoyed having missionaries stay at their home for extended times of rest. Because he was wealthy, he financially supported a mission in India, missionaries, native preachers, and an orphanage.

Virginia's teenage years were made difficult because her body remained frail. Adding to her weakened condition, at the age of thirteen she suffered a fall that damaged her spine. Undeterred, she finished high school and was in college when her father took ill. She stopped her studies to assist her mother with her father's care. Near death, one day her father asked his wife to pray with him. She wanted to call a minister, but he insisted that she was the right person to pray for him because "she had prayed many years for his conversion, now she must help or no one could." Virginia's father gave his heart to Jesus, and after a time went home to be with the Lord on April 18, 1892.

Virginia married on December 18, 1893, and soon a son was born to the young couple. In December 1900 Virginia gave birth to a daughter, but the baby died within forty-eight hours of her birth. In March of the following year, Virginia took ill and almost died. In June 1902, she gave birth to a second son, and she became partially paralyzed from the stress of childbirth on her injured spine. Within a short time she was completely paralyzed, and spent a year at the Clifton Springs Sanitarium in New York. In July 1904, Virginia was returned to her childhood home for continued care. Upon hearing that her mother's health had taken a turn for the worse, Virginia was in anguish, and her own body's condition worsened to the point that she was given five hours to live. She survived, however, and spent the next months reflecting on the Scriptures, and after a time said "Yes" to God's call upon her life to teach and preach his Word.

On December 13, 1904, Virginia was miraculously healed. "The Holy Spirit came upon me and shook me so that the bed moved, windows and walls and floors rattled and my soul was flooded with joy. The fire of the Holy Ghost enveloped me . . . My limbs that had been lifeless, now bounded with life and I heard God saying to me, 'Arise and walk.'"[3] Not only did Virginia experience personal healing and victory, but as news spread of her healing, a revival spread in her town. Individuals were converted, some recommitted their lives to Christ, and others experienced sanctification and divine healing.

Initially, her testimony was well received by Virginia's Methodist pastor and church congregation. His support, however, soon turned to opposition and ridicule because if he wholly embraced Virginia's message, "his church would be overturned and driven to repentance, and he himself would be convicted of having grieved the Holy Spirit and of not feeding the flock nor preaching the whole truth."[4] Although she continued to attend the church for another year, she began to hold home prayer meetings with her husband's support. An itinerant ministry unfolded as

---

3. Ibid., 16.
4. Ibid., 18.

Virginia began holding prayer meetings in surrounding cities, and sharing her testimony and teaching God's Word.

In January 1906 Virginia and Sister Tozer, a coworker, went to pray for a sick woman in New Durham, New Jersey. The woman experienced both salvation and divine healing and told them that God had instructed her to give up her room so that Virginia could start a mission in the city. As confirmation that God was in the founding of the mission, one woman provided chairs, two brothers volunteered to paint the walls, another woman gave money for bedding, and others contributed toward the purchase of an organ. On the evening of February 7, 1906, the rescue mission was opened and was named the Door of Hope Mission. Its focus was evangelism, faith healing, and care for prostitutes. Virginia continued to share her testimony and assist with services in other cities. This included meetings of the Missionary Alliance in New York, and other cities around the state. In some cities, she held three services a day.

Through reading the teachings regarding "latter rain" in Carrie Judd Montgomery's *The Triumphs of Faith*, Virginia began to seek a deeper experience in the Holy Spirit. Although Pentecostalism experienced a stirring of the Holy Spirit in the 1940s that bore the name "Latter Rain," the term originally derived from a movement that began at the beginning of the twentieth century. Within this context, "Latter Rain"[56] referred to an interpretation of Joel 2:23 in which the "former" (or "early") rain was the outpouring of the Holy Spirit as recorded in Acts 2, and the "latter rain" was the outpouring of the Holy Spirit in the beginning of the twentieth century.

This interpretation became an apologetic for Pentecostalism since the moving of the Spirit within Pentecostalism was contrary to the teachings of dispensationalism, which was prevalent in the Christian church at the time. Contrary to dispensational teachings, the gifts of the Holy Spirit were presently in operation rather than having ceased at the end of the Apostolic Age, and the church was experiencing a reinvigoration by the Spirit rather than following a trajectory of spiritual decline as was taught in dispensationalism.

Members of the mission traveled to Nyack in the summer of 1907, and a number of them received the Pentecostal experience of Spirit bap-

---

5. White, *Acts of the Apostles*, 55.
6. Robeck, *Azusa Street*, 235.

tism, accompanied by speaking in tongues at prayer meetings held there. Upon their return, Virginia and others received this experience during services at the mission. The year 1909 was significant in Virginia's ministry for two reasons. First, as a foundation step toward answering God's leading to expand, the ministry was incorporated on February 1 and its name was changed from the Door of Hope to the Church of Jesus. Secondly, on April 1, Virginia opened a "Rest Home" (faith home). Although faith homes predated Pentecostalism, within the context of the emerging Pentecostal movement these homes were "facilities in which groups of Christian workers under the supervision of acknowledged leaders lived and ministered."[7] Eventually, the church's name was changed to Beulah Heights Assembly when it was moved to North Bergen, New Jersey.

As the world's need for the gospel was very real to her, Virginia opened the Beulah Heights Bible and Missionary Training School in 1912 in North Bergen.[8] Although she was aware of the anti-intellectualism of Pentecostals, she was guided by Paul's admonition to Timothy to "study to show yourself approved unto God . . ." (2 Timothy 2:15). The last school event Virginia attended was Beulah's seventh graduation ceremony. By that time, graduates of the school were serving as pastors and evangelists in the United States and as missionaries to India, Africa, China, Japan, Palestine, Puerto Rico, and South America. Among Beulah's early graduates were a number of Assemblies of God foreign missionaries, including Edgar Barrick (India), Fred Burke (South Africa), Henry B. Garlock (Africa), Frank Finkenbinder (Latin America), John Juergensen (Japan) and Marie Stephany (North China).[9]

Virginia went home to be with the Lord on June 28, 1919. In keeping with the legacy of 2 Timothy 1:5, at the time of her death her one son who was still living was serving as a pastor of a Pentecostal church in Bridgeport, Connecticut.

---

7. Blumhofer, "Life on the Faith Lines," 11.
8. McGee, "Three Notable Women," 12.
9. McGee, "Virginia E. Moss," 909.

17

Her Tongue Talked Fluently in a Language She Had Never Learned

Minnie Tingley Draper

"GOD WANTS THE VERY best of you—all there is—and wants it now. Will you say, 'Yes, Lord,' and enter the arms wide-stretched to you? Will you give Him today what He wants—your heart, your will, to satisfy His desire?"[1] These words, written by Minnie Tingley Draper in the "Young People's Work" column of *The Christian Alliance and Foreign Missionary Weekly*, were as much words of advice to young people as they were representative of her life and testimony.

Minnie was born in Waquit, Massachusetts, and grew up in Ossinging, New York. Raised by an unemployed single mother, as a young adult Minnie provided financially for their home through teaching. In matters of faith, Minnie was a Presbyterian and an active churchgoer. Eventually, the teaching load Minnie carried led to a breakdown in her health to the point that she became an invalid.

Although a number of physicians were consulted, her physical suffering continued.

Having run out of medical options, Minnie heard about miraculous cures that were part of the growing divine healing (also known as the "faith cure") movement. Hoping for an answer, she traveled to New York to attend services at Albert Benjamin (A. B.) Simpson's Faith Tabernacle. Typically, on Wednesday afternoons services were held at the Tabernacle

---

1. Draper, "God's Desire," 547.

for "the deepening of the spiritual life and divine healing."[2] This would be followed by an anointing service for healing at Simpson's Berachah ("Valley of Blessing") Home. It is likely that in just such a service Minnie was anointed with oil and a prayer was said for her healing. She was instantly healed, and simultaneously the Lord "definitely sanctified and anointed her with the Holy Ghost and power."[3] As a result of her healing, she adopted the belief in Christ as healer shared by Simpson and the adherents in the Christian and Missionary Alliance (CMA). For the rest of her life she relied on the Lord for healing and never again took any medicine or visited any doctors.

Simpson had opened the Berachah Home on May 1, 1883, in his home at 331 West 34th Street in Manhattan. Although the Home was moved to new locations as its ministry expanded, its purpose remained the same. According to Simpson, "it affords to persons seeking a deeper spiritual life or divine healing, a season of entire rest, seclusion from the distractions of their ordinary life, and often from uncongenial surroundings." Once healed, individuals would encourage other residents by sharing their testimonies of healing. Now healthy, Draper became a very successful evangelist and was known for her prayers for the sick. This included ministry in the Berachah Home, as Minnie was among those listed as having been "much used of the Lord"[4] there.

For many years Minnie worked with A. B. Simpson, assisting with his conventions in Rock Springs, Pennsylvania, New York City, and Old Orchard, Maine. A 1906 report on the Maine convention indicated that Minnie's teaching on divine healing, along with that of Miss Lindenberger, was so captivating that "it kept the leaders engaged through the entire afternoon."[5] She also served on the executive board of the Christian and Missionary Alliance until it was reorganized in 1912, and was a writer for the organization's publications. Of commitment to the Lord she wrote, "Whatever it means, will you let the dear Lord have all He wants? If you do, you will be met; for 'Thou satisfiest the desire of every living thing,' and every yearning of your soul to be good and useful will be accomplished,

---

2. Curtis, *Faith in the Great Physician*, 153.
3. Lucas, "In Memoriam," 3.
4. Thompson, *Life of A. B. Simpson*, 143.
5. "Old Orchard Convention," 125.

because you are in close touch with Jesus."[6] In a 1910 convention of the Boston branch of the CMA, she was responsible for conducting the daily "quiet hour."

When she heard of the Azusa Street Revival and the events that were part of the new Pentecostal movement, she was in somewhat of a dilemma. On the one hand, she was cautious regarding these new spiritual manifestations, and on the other, she was seeking a greater work of the Holy Spirit in her life. Always devout, she wanted a deeper walk with the Lord. While in prayer alone in her room the Lord appeared to her and "hours elapsed wherein she saw unutterable things, and when she finally came to herself, she heard her tongue talking fluently in a language she had never learned."[7]

Her Pentecostal experience would have an immediate negative impact on her ministry within the CMA. Those who did not agree with the new doctrine, which taught that speaking in tongues is "initial evidence" that a person is baptized in the Holy Spirit, grew suspicious of Minnie. As a result, her preaching opportunities within the denomination were curtailed. Yet in adopting this new experience, Minnie was not alone within the CMA. In fact, at one point there were so many people experiencing Spirit baptism that some thought the CMA was now a Pentecostal denomination. However, the CMA did not embrace this new experience and many individuals left the denomination. Minnie, although identifying with adherents of the Pentecostal movement, remained active in the CMA until 1913.

An early step in Minnie's ministry within the Pentecostal movement was to help organize and then lead the Bethel Pentecostal Assembly in Newark, New Jersey. In 1909 the Assembly sent out George Bowie as a missionary to South Africa. The following year, Bowie founded the Pentecostal Mission there, which would later become the Full Gospel Church of God in Southern Africa, a bilingual church. Although Minnie branched out in other ventures for the Lord, she continued to serve as president of the Bethel board.

The second church Minnie was instrumental in organizing was the Ossining Gospel Assembly in Ossining, New York, which was begun in 1913. During its early years a number of significant individuals in the

---

6. Draper, "God's Desire," 547.
7. Lucas, "In Memoriam," 3.

Pentecostal movement served at the church, some as interim pastors. These included Frank M. Boyd, Robert A. Brown, William I. Evans, Christian J. Lucas, David McDowell, Harry J. Steil, Allen A. Swift, and Ernest S. Williams.

It was through Bethel however, the first church she organized, that Minnie would have a significant impact on Pentecostal missions. "In 1910 the Executive Council of the Bethel Pentecostal Assembly, Inc., organized 'to maintain and conduct a general evangelistic work in the State of New Jersey, in all other states of the United States and any and all foreign countries.'"[8] Although institutions founded by the board were independent, a number of the staff held credentials with the Assemblies of God. By the 1920s the Bethel church became a center for mission conventions and a great source of financial backing for missionaries. One writer in *The Latter Rain Evangel* noted that at Bethel "it was a common thing to receive as much as seven to eight thousand dollars in a single missionary offering."[9]

The board sent missionaries to China, India, South Africa, and South America. These included Ralph (who later served as general superintendent of the Assemblies of God in 1953–59) and Lillian Riggs, George and Eleanor Bowie, and Edgar and Mabel Pettenger. The *South and Central African Missionary Herald* (later the *Full Gospel Missionary Herald*) was published to keep constituents and donors informed about the missions activities of the board. Minnie was a significant person in the development of Pentecostal mission as she "served as the president of the first major Pentecostal missions agency, called the 'Bethel Board,' until her death in 1921."[10]

Minnie's impact on Pentecostal missions increased in 1916 when she founded the Bethel Bible Training School in Newark, New Jersey. The school was patterned after the Missionary Training School (MTS) founded by A. B. Simpson, and some MTS graduates became part of the faculty in this new academic endeavor. William W. Simpson, a former CMA missionary to China and Tibet who joined the Assemblies of God, Frank M. Boyd, and William I. Evans served as deans of the school. Among the

---

8. McGee, "Three Notable Women," 4.
9. Ibid.
10. Robert, *American Women in Mission*, 251.

school's graduates were Thomas Brubaker, Howard Osgood, and Paul and Dorothy Emery, who became prominent in the Assemblies of God.

It is significant to note that the Rochester Bible Training School (1906), the Bethel Bible Training School (1916), and Glad Tidings Bible Institute (1919), all founded by women, "supplied missionary candidates for the Assemblies of God"[11] in its earliest years. Women provided a pivotal foundation of the missional work of not only the Assemblies of God, but in the Pentecostal movement as a whole. "When examining the role of women in early Pentecostal missions, it quickly becomes apparent that women provided vital leadership in the areas of missiological reflection, mission education and mission administration. In the first generation, Pentecostal missions were an outgrowth of the premillenial, holiness, healing milieu that was so dominated by women at the turn of the century."[12]

For women, the empowerment to take on the challenges of their ministerial, educational, and administrative work came through the experience of Spirit baptism. Their Holiness background, in part because it included experiences of divine healing, enabled them to adopt a paradigm in which works of God such as divine healing and Spirit baptism were available in the current era and did not cease at the close of the Apostolic Age. Minnie was just such a woman, having been raised a Presbyterian, later experiencing divine healing and sanctification in the Christian Missionary Alliance, and finally, as a result of experiencing Spirit baptism, giving her "very best" in establishing churches, a missions agency, and a Christian college.

---

11. McGee, "This Gospel Shall be Preached," 6–7.
12. Robert, *American Women in Mission*, 252.

18

Going Where She Thought a Man Should Go

Nora Chambers

FIVE FOUNDING MOTHERS, ADELINE and Madeline Lauftus, Melinda and Polly Plemons, and Barbara Spurling, joined three founding fathers, John Plemons Jr., John Plemons Sr., and Richard Spurling, in answering the call to form the Christian Union on August 19, 1886. Organized at the call of Richard Green Spurling, this church was based on "four tenets: a desire to be free from man-made creeds and traditions; a willingness to accept the New Testament as their only rule of faith; a commitment to give each other equal rights and privileges to read and interpret Scripture; and a willingness to sit together as the church of God to transact business."[1]

Before forming this "New Testament church," Richard G. Spurling and his father both had served as Baptist ministers primarily in the Unicoi Mountains of eastern Tennessee. While serving at the Pleasant Hill Baptist Church in Cherokee County, North Carolina, "R.G.," the younger Spurling, became disaffected with the Landmark Baptists, the predominant Christian group in the area. The distinctive beliefs of the Landmark Baptists included the historic "Baptist succession" traced back by contemporary Baptists to John the Baptist; the visible, local congregation as the only "church" (there is no spiritual, universal church spanning the globe); and Communion being restricted to members of each local Baptist church. Ultimately, the Baptists revoked Spurling's ministerial license and church membership.

---

1. Dirksen, "Let Your Women Keep Silence," 168.

A month after its formation, R. G. Spurling was chosen to pastor the Christian Union Church, which ordained him on September 26, 1886. Over the next few years, congregations were added to this new organization. The Christian Union was destined to be yet another small indigenous church group except for a Holiness revival in 1896. The revival was led by Fire-Baptized Holiness evangelists William Martin, Joe M. Tipton, and Milton McNabb, and held in the Shearer Schoolhouse in Coker Creek County, Tennessee. "An unusual feature of the this revival was the fact that several of those who received sanctification reportedly spoke in tongues when they 'prayed through.' This manifestation, which seemed strange to mountain folk, caused great excitement in the community."[2]

Among those seeking sanctification at the revival was William Franklin Bryant, a lay leader in the Liberty Baptist Church. After much prayer, and laying his life "on the altar," he experienced sanctification one morning while sitting on horseback. Bryant then became a leader in this congregation of Holiness people. Emboldened by their experiences in the revival, they started preaching sanctification in their largely Baptist and Methodist environs.

The reaction to this new doctrine was swift and increasingly violent. Members of the Christian Union soon discovered the Shearer Schoolhouse bolted shut, and they were forbidden to hold any more services there. In response, Richard Kilpatrick donated some of his land for them to build a church, and a rough structure made of logs was erected. What followed were investigations and church discipline for those who had not left their original churches. Then there were attempts to disrupt the Holiness services with shouting and gun blasts, one of which wounded Bryant. Finally a mob of 106 people burnt down the church where the Holiness meetings were being held. With this last destructive act, the larger community and local law enforcement stepped in to help stop the violence.

What followed was what Church of God historian Dr. Charles Conn called "fanaticism." This included fasting for interminable time periods, which negatively affected people's health, multiple baptisms in the Spirit with names like "Holy Dynamite," "Holy Lyditte," and "Holy Oxidite," and a teaching that believers were incapable of sinning once they were baptized in the Holy Spirit. In response, R. G. Spurling called a meeting at Bryant's home on May 15, 1902. At this meeting, the church was "reorganized . . .

---

2. Synan, *Holiness-Pentecostal Tradition*, 72.

with a simple plan of government designed to safeguard the group from future interlopers."[3] The group also changed its name from the Christian Union to the Holiness Church of Camp Creek.

The church stabilized over the next year, and then in 1903 there was a new arrival who would chart a new national and eventually an international path for the church. Ambrose Jessup Tomlinson, raised a Quaker, was born in rural Indiana. He was a colporteur (traveling Bible salesperson) for the American Bible Society and his route took him from Maine to Georgia. Tomlinson had been in attendance at the 1896 Camp Creek revival. He was also strongly influenced by the writings of Carrie Judd Montgomery about the doctrine of divine healing. In 1903 Tomlinson relocated his family to Culbertson, North Carolina, and continued his work for the American Bible Society. He soon joined up with the Holiness Church of Camp Creek and was ordained on June 13, 1903.

In 1906, the first general assembly of the Holiness Church was held, and of the twenty-one delegates, seven were women. At the second general assembly, held at the Union Grove meeting house, ten miles from Cleveland, Tennessee, the name Church of God was adopted for the denomination. A point of concern at this assembly was that the majority of delegates were women. Concerns were abated when "the important positions occupied by women in the time of Christ and His apostles"[4] were pointed out. The 1914 Church of God general assembly proved pivotal for both Tomlinson and the denomination. A message delivered in tongues, with interpretation, confirmed Tomlinson's appointment as general overseer of the denomination into perpetuity. Tomlinson not only led the expansive growth of the Church of God, and structured a strong organizational foundation for the denomination, but also provided the biblical/theological framework for restrictions on women in ministry and church/denominational polity that continue to the present day.

Nora Chambers became a member of the Church of God in 1910 when Richard G. Spurling convinced her that the denomination was "the true Bible Church."[5] She was also licensed that year as an evangelist, with "authority to publish, preach and defend the Gospel of Jesus

---

3. Conn, *Like a Mighty Army*, 45.
4. "Church of God General Assembly Minutes," 20.
5. Carroll, "Youth Interviews Experience," 14.

Christ, to baptize, to administer the Lord's Supper and the washing of the Saints feet."[6]

The following year, Nora and her husband, Fred, worked at Holmes Bible School (HBS) in Greenville, South Carolina, and Nora was one of its teachers. In their second year there, she and her husband teamed up with evangelist E. J. Boehmer to take a group of students from HBS to preach in North Carolina and Georgia. This was a special time for Nora, although they were operating with little financial resources and faced mounting resistance to their ministry in the area. Of this time she wrote, "When God was dearest to me was when I spent two years of persecution in the mountains of North Carolina and Georgia. We were attending Holmes' Bible School at Altamont, South Carolina, when the Lord led a little band of students from the school to this section of the country. They had not heard about holiness. They were taught that no one could live above sin and our teaching was considered false teaching. When the cream of the churches accepted this doctrine they thought we were tearing up their churches and this brought persecution."[7]

As churches in the area started to adopt the doctrine of holiness, the persecution intensified. This included the threat of being tarred and feathered, the house they were living in being pelted with rocks, gunshots aimed in the direction of the services, and Nora's husband being beaten by a group of masked men.[8]

Because of her writing ability and education, Nora was selected as proofreader for the Church of God Publishing House when it opened in 1917. This year would be important for Nora in another significant way, as it was then that the Church of God General Overseer, A. J. "Tomlinson proposed a Bible Training School for the purpose of equipping men and women in 'Bible and missionary training.' The Assembly voted to establish a school with Tomlinson as Superintendent; but he appointed Nora Chambers, a woman who was a licensed evangelist, as the primary teacher."[9]

Nora resisted the appointment as she thought she was of the wrong gender to take the position. "I insisted that a man should be chosen for that

---

6. "Church of God Evangelist's License," 1.
7. "When God Was Dearest to Me," 14.
8. Chambers, "Brief Sketch of Our Work," 26, 29–30.
9. Alexander and Gause, *Women in Leadership*, 16.

position, but finally consented when all my suggestions met opposition."[10] In contrast so Nora's self-assessment, Church of God historian Charles Conn concluded that Nora was "a woman of rare intelligence, ability and, for that early day, education . . . an altruistic and tireless woman, seeking to help and encourage others at all times. It was natural that she should be selected as the first teacher for the new school, but, in keeping with her unassuming disposition, she at first insisted that a man be made instructor. Her modesty, while sincere, was never a mark of timidity."[11]

The appointment was significant as the denomination, guided by Tomlinson's interpretation of the council of Jerusalem in (Acts 15:1–35), increasingly structured in restrictions on women in ministry and church governance. Tomlinson's legacy continues today within the Church of God in the unequal opportunities women have to participate in the leadership within the denomination. Even the original ministerial duties in Nora's Evangelist License granted in 1910 were subject to give and take for women over the decades that followed.

The Bible Training School opened on New Year's Day 1918 with twelve students—five men and seven women—with Nora as the sole teacher. The school was originally housed in the second floor of the building at 2524 Gaut Street, Cleveland, out which *Evangel*, the denominational magazine, was published. As for the school's curriculum, "The Bible shall be the principle textbook, but such literary work and music as is necessary shall be included in the course."

Students taught by Nora include L. C. Chambers, Hallie Chesser, Jessie Danehower, E. M. Ellis, C. J. Hindmon, John C. Jernigan, Joe Little, Zeno C. Tharp, Paul Walker, and Grant Williams, all outstanding leaders of the Church of God.

In later years, Nora and her husband were involved in the missionary efforts of the Church of God in the Caribbean.[12] Her work in publications included assisting Alda B. Harrison with *The Lighted Pathway*, the official Church of God youth publication founded by Harrison in 1929. Nora served three years as editor of the "Children's Page." Additionally, for four years she wrote the weekly Bible lessons for *Junior Jewels*. A compassionate woman, Nora also served as matron of an orphanage for four years.

---

10. "Youth Interviews Experience," 14.
11. Conn, *Like a Mighty Army*, 148–49.
12. Conn, *Where the Saints Have Trod*, 57.

She remained active in the North Cleveland Church of God. Because of health concerns, she eventually moved to Phoenix, Arizona, where she went to be with the Lord in 1953.

19

Suffering at the Hands of Revisionist Historians

Mary Craig

Another way of writing the word "history" is "his story." In the area of gender, women's roles in the founding of institutions are sometimes given a subordinate role or erased altogether. This is a truism within both secular and religious realms.

In gathering source material for this chapter, the researcher came across an Assemblies of God news release entitled, "Bethany College: 85 years aflame."[1] Part of the release reads as follows: "The 2004–2005 academic year marks the 85th year of Bethany College, the Assemblies of God's oldest college and the first Pentecostal institution of higher education in the United States. What began as one man's vision had evolved into a history of leadership interwoven with the rise of worldwide Pentecostalism. Founded as Glad Tidings Bible Institute in 1919 by Robert Craig Jr. . . ."[2] The Web site of Glad Tidings Church provides a little more accurate tribute to the founding of the school: "The success of Glad Tidings Bible Institute began by Sister Craig to establish new converts in the faith and qualify aspiring workers in the Word, led to the purchase of property and construction of the six-story building."[3]

One fateful day in 1911, Robert Craig met Mrs. Mary McCullough, a married immigrant from Denmark, during services held by a Congregational minister in a San Francisco church. Robert, a former Methodist

---

1. "Bethany College: 85 years Aflame," 1.
2. Ibid.
3. Glad Tidings Church, "Our History."

minister and now a committed Pentecostal, was returning to the city in which he had suffered much tragedy. In 1904, his wife died in childbirth after two years of marriage. At the time he was serving as an assistant minister in a Methodist church. A second tragedy struck in the form of the San Francisco earthquake of 1906, and a resultant fire left half of the church's 800-member congregation homeless. Then in his late thirties, Robert suffered a nervous breakdown, and he gave up active ministry and left San Francisco for Southern California.

Four years later Robert's physical and emotional health had still not improved. God, however, had a spiritual solution for his ailments. On a Pacific Electric Railway System ride from Compton to Los Angeles, Robert met Mr. and Mrs. J. Finley Berry, who invited him to a service at the Pentecostal mission on South Spring Street. At the service he was both miraculously healed and baptized in the Holy Spirit. Of the experience he would later write, "here was something of which we proud Methodists of the early twentieth century knew nothing, though I now know that in his day John Wesley understood it . . . In the fullness of time, when I was ready to receive healing from heaven, God led me to those despised Pentecostal people, catching me as it were by guile, but I am one of them—Glory!"[4]

A few days later he accepted another invitation from the Berrys to share with them a Sunday meal and devotion at their country home. During the devotion time Robert was "slain in the Spirit" (falling to the ground under the influence of the Holy Spirit). Over the next few days of devoted prayer, God called Robert to return to San Francisco and gave him the promise that if he would be obedient, his ministry would yield 100,000 souls for the kingdom. Upon his return to San Francisco, Robert started a rescue mission on Post Street. Three months later, he leased a building that had previously housed the O'Farrell Street Jim Corbett Saloon to provide a larger space for the mission. Those who came to the mission for sustenance partook of a menu that consisted of fish, fish heads, fish tails, stale bread, and discarded vegetables.

Mrs. Mary McCullough was a hardworking woman who had a passion for preaching to homeless men in her neighborhood who were suffering from alcohol abuse. About the same time that Robert moved the mission to its O'Farrell Street location, Mary's husband died. She then became very involved with the work of the mission with "fervency and

---

4. Wilson, "Robert J. Craig's Glad Tidings," 9.

commitment." Eventually a romance bloomed, and on April 23, 1913, Robert and Mary were married on her birthday. Of his marriage to Mary, Robert later commented that he was glad he had "waited for Sister Craig eight and a half years ... I am glad I did wait. What a loss we should have suffered had I not waited for her."[5]

By 1915 Robert and Mary were able to secure property at 1536 Ellis Street, and this became home to church later known as "Old Glad Tidings." As the Bay Area was increasingly the midpoint in the crossroads of Pentecostalism in Northern California, it is not surprising that Glad Tidings became a center for the Pentecostal movement. In 1916 Maria Woodworth-Etter conducted an extended evangelistic campaign, and the attendance outgrew the mission building to the point that the revival services were continued in the 1500-seat National Theater. Three years later Aimee Semple McPherson crossed the Bay Bridge from Oakland into San Francisco riding in her famous "Gospel Car" to conduct evangelistic services at the mission. According to Robert, the effect of this campaign was that "literally towering mountains of prejudice against the Pentecostal movement have been swept away under the same candid and forceful presentation of the Full Gospel Message."[6]

The impetus to begin the new converts class that eventually become Bethany University was the conversion of "Brother Richards" from spiritualism. Mary had become concerned about the lapses men experienced in their faith walk after their conversion at the mission. Moving forward with the assurance of the Lord that "the Word will keep them," in May of 1918 she began a new converts class in the kitchen of their second story apartment at the mission. According to Mary, "I began Glad Tidings Bible Training Institute with only two students and one of them was drunk."[7] The first lesson was about sacrificial blood in the Old Testament in the context of the account of Cain and Abel. By October attendance had grown to eighteen, and by Christmas one hundred students were in attendance at the nightly sessions.

The school, originally named the Pacific Bible Institute, was formally opened on October 6, 1919, when a systematic two-year curriculum was offered for daytime students. The original school faculty consisted of

5. Ibid., 73.
6. Ibid., 87.
7. Ibid., 100.

Mary (who also cooked for the resident students), affectionately known to the students as "Auntie May"; Ira Surface, a former Presbyterian minister who experienced Spirit baptism following his divine healing; Mrs. Surface, a former public school teacher, who taught English; Florence Murcutt, a Jewish medical doctor from Australia; and Lillian Yeomans, also a physician. Robert would eventually serve as "superintendent" and devotional leader. In his administrative role Robert recruited Daniel W. Kerr and William Peirce to help structure the school. Alice Luce, who founded the Latin American Bible Institute, taught at Glad Tidings in the 1920s and 30s.

When the original twelve students of the daytime academic program completed the two-year course of study in 1921, Mary gave each graduate a Scripture verse she felt was appropriate for that individual. This was a tradition that would continue in the school into the 1950s. The school was soon renamed the Glad Tidings Bible Institute. In its second year of operation, thirty-five students were enrolled in the daytime program and the evening classes grew significantly. Initially, apartments across the street from the mission were rented to accommodate the growing enrollment. In its early years, attendance at the school cost $0.75 a day for "room, board and tuition." It was also not unusual for "outpourings of the Holy Spirit" to interrupt the proceedings of campus events. As Mary and Robert were friends of George and Carrie Judd Montgomery, Carrie publicized proceedings at the school in her *Triumphs of Faith* publication.

The school's location was ideal for students to engage in urban ministry. The program of the school "integrated local evangelism with classroom studies. Its academic component essentially expanded on the subject matter one encountered in Pentecostal sermons and Sunday Schools. That was considered sufficient, not only because few Pentecostal educators had more to offer, but also because the prevalent Pentecostal mind-set distained formal training as potentially 'quenching the Spirit.'"[8]

Robert and Mary continued to work through the Glad Tidings Church and Bible Institute, and later a radio station, towards the fulfillment of original vision of reaching 100,000 souls. According to the seventy-fifth commemorative book of Bethany University (the school Glad Tidings Bible Institute would become), "the founder's vision for reaching 100,000 souls with the gospel . . . finds its greatest meaning in

---

8. Blumhofer, *Assemblies of God*, 315–16.

his strategy for establishing a school."⁹ Wayne Warner, in an article about Robert's support of Maria B. Woodworth-Etter's ministry, wrote, "another early Pentecostal leader, Robert J. Craig, pastor of Glad Tidings Temple, San Francisco, and the founder of what is now Bethany Bible College." These assertions are at variance with the school's early publications. In the 1937 *Tidings* yearbook of the Glad Tidings Bible Institute, the editors wrote, "It was upon this Scripture that our beloved founder, Sister Robert J. Craig, nineteen years ago saw the need of some method of rooting and grounding new converts in the Lord . . . she realized that a convert class was needed. One was immediately started which provided a good beginning for such a spiritual school as Glad Tidings Bible Institute, the school of prayer."¹⁰

Within Pentecostalism there was a tradition of attributing to men new works of God established by women. One version of this phenomenon is that the founding of a church (or churches) planted by a woman is attributed to a male pastor assigned once the congregation was organized into a church. In other cases, among married couples, the wives tended to demure to their husbands and allow them to get the credit for ministerial endeavors accomplished by either both of them or by her. This latter was not the case with Mary Craig. As was the practice within Bible institute/college publications of that era, the 1938 Glad Tidings Bible Institute *Tidings* yearbook includes a "A Word from the Founder" page . . . and Mary is the only person on it. The following is "her story," taken from that page recounting the founding of the school.

"While meditating upon the dangerous position in this world of uninstructed babes in Christ, God revealed to me the great need of a new converts Bible class. One was immediately started which provided a good beginning for such a spiritual school as Glad Tidings Bible Institute, the school of prayer.

"In the year of 1918 the converts class, as it was called, met in the kitchen during the regular Sunday School session. Because of such interest this group of six grew to eighteen by October of 1919, five months after its beginning, and at Christmas there were one hundred enrolled. Bro. Craig acted as the superintendent in the years to follow which resulted in a great spiritual atmosphere to prevail . . . the first class graduated in 1921. Out of

---

9. Wilson and Little, *75 Years of Dreams*, 21.

10. "The Word Will Keep Them." *Tidings of 1937*. San Francisco, CA: Glad Tidings Bible Institute (1937) 6–7.

this initial class of twelve, six became missionaries, and one of them was Sister Tennant who went to Alaska and later came home to fill a need here at the Institute and Temple."[11]

---

11. Craig, "Word from the Founder," 5.

20

A Gifted and Flamboyant Founder

AIMEE SEMPLE MCPHERSON

>Churchgoers entered the sanctuary to see illustrated across the back of the stage a long winding road with a lone cross standing at an intersection. On the platform stood a police motorcycle, McPherson wearing a badge, an officer's cap, and a policewoman's uniform and skirt, completed the scene.
>
>She began the sermon justifying a motorcycle in church. "If Christ were alive today, I think he'd preach modern parables about oil wells and airplanes, the things that you and I understand. Things like being arrested for speeding."
>
>Then, in an instant, she flipped on the motorcycle siren, letting it wail while the audience gasped. Nobody dozed off during that service focusing on individuals' need for salvation.[1]

THE JOURNEY TO THIS dramatic event begins in desolate Canadian countryside near Ingersoll, Ontario. On October 9, 1890, Aimee Elizabeth was born to James Kennedy and his second wife Mildred (Millie). Her birth was an answer to her mother's prayer. Having read the biblical account of Hannah and the birth of Hannah's son Samuel, Millie began praying for a daughter that she could dedicate to the Lord. When Aimee was born, Millie sat by the window of her home and "her lips softly paraphrased the scripture [1 Samuel 1:11] which had become a part of her very life: 'For this child I prayed; and the Lord gave me my petition,

---

1. Sutton, *Aimee Semple McPherson*, 72.

which I asked of him. Therefore also I have lent her unto the Lord; as long as she liveth she shall be lent unto the Lord.'"[2]

Growing up, Aimee had the double influence of Methodism and the Salvation Army. Her father, a farmer and bridge builder by trade, was a Methodist organist and choir director. It was from him that she learned to play piano and organ. Her mother was a dedicated officer of the Salvation Army, serving as the Sergeant Major of the Ingersoll corps.

Minnie made the daily trek by foot or by sleigh to the Army barracks, where her tasks included making sure operations went smoothly, coordinating church services when higher ranking officers were not present, and serving as correspondent with headquarters. At the same time, she ensured that her household was taken care of and that all chores were completed.

Throughout her childhood, Aimee's mother made sure that she was spiritually nurtured and immersed in the life and ministry of the Salvation Army. This included attendance at "prayer meetings (knee drills), holiness meetings, street meetings, Band of Love gatherings, regular sieges (concentrated days of prayer or work), and entertainments . . . teas, jam tart hallelujahs (socials with refreshments), self-denial weeks, and a seemingly endless round of lectures and recitations on such varied themes as 'What is Canada Noted For,' 'How the Post Office Works,' and the Bible."[3]

Along with opportunities for spiritual and social growth, Aimee also came in contact with the dramatic enactments that were an integral part of the preaching of Evangeline Booth, the famed evangelist and daughter of William and Catherine Booth, the founders of the Salvation Army. Aimee was able to experience firsthand how powerful and effective drama could be, especially when utilized to deliver the gospel message.

Aimee's public speaking skills found early development during her membership in the Loyal, Temperance Legion, the children's arm of the Woman's Christian Temperance Union. On various occasions she spoke on temperance in religious, social, and political settings. Her ability in public speaking was recognized in the medals she earned for her elocution.

On a personal level, growing up in the sometimes rugged circumstances of the Canadian outback had a strong influence on Aimee's interests and character. She learned "self-reliance and toughness while

---

2. McPherson, *Story of My Life*, 16.
3. Blumhofer, *Aimee Semple McPherson*, 46.

A Gifted and Flamboyant Founder

cultivating a love for the outdoors, and delight in a good challenge, too. This upbringing became a source of pride that would be a constant reference point throughout her life."[4]

When she reached her teenage years, Aimee attended the Ingersoll Collegiate High School with its rigorous curriculum in English, French, history, literature, mathematics, and the sciences. It was through her study of science that Aimee's faith in God's existence was shaken for a time, when she was taught the theory of evolution.

During the winter of 1907–1908, Aimee was scheduled to lead the first ice waltz at a local carnival but her parents insisted that she attend a revival meeting. They compromised and Aimee was to attend the service after her performance. Although she stood at the back of the meeting hall, the evangelist's daughter approached her and challenged Aimee about her faith. Although she insisted that because of her belief in evolution she couldn't be a Christian, Aimee's heart had nevertheless been stirred. Upon her return home, she found a quiet spot, kneeled, and prayed, "O God . . . if there is a God . . . reveal yourself to me!"[5]

The answer to that prayer came in the form of "Irish Evangelist" Robert James Semple, who was holding a series of storefront revival meetings in Ingersoll. Using Acts 2:38–39 as his text, Semple preached a sermon that convicted Aimee and she was able to make a firm commitment to the Lord. She would also experience the baptism of the Holy Spirit accompanied by speaking in tongues.

After a brief courtship, Aimee and Robert were wed on August 12, 1908, in a Salvation Army ceremony. Initially settling in Stratford, Ontario, they soon moved to London, Ontario. Robert and Aimee were then ordained by William H. Durham and assisted Durham with evangelistic tours in the northern United States and in Canada. "It was under Durham's tutelage that Aimee discovered she had the gift of interpretation of tongues, a gift she exercised with frequency and eloquence for many years."[6]

In 1910 the young couple then began the missionary trip to China they had envisioned when they married. Their itinerary included Ireland, England, and a trip through the Suez Canal, before reaching their final

---

4. Sutton, *Aimee Semple McPherson*, 9.
5. McPherson, *Story of My Life*, 28.
6. Blumhofer, *Aimee Semple McPherson*, 81.

destination of Hong Kong. Robert and Aimee immediately immersed themselves in language studies, but unfortunately within weeks of their arrival in Hong Kong Robert died of malaria.

Pregnant and with few financial resources, Aimee remained in Hong Kong until her daughter Roberta Star was born on September 17, 1910. She then joined her mother in New York and began work with the Salvation Army. While there she met Harold Stewart McPherson, whom she married on October 24, 1911. They settled in Providence, Rhode Island, and in 1913 their son son, Rolf Potter, was born.

The McPherson family then relocated to Canada where Aimee and Harold ministered together. Harold would handle all the logistics of the evangelistic meetings and Aimee would preach. In 1917 Aimee began publishing *The Bridal Call*, a monthly magazine she used to share her teaching. This type of publication was used by evangelists of this era to build and sustain the interest of the minister's constituency, and this was also the case with *The Bridal Call*. However, the rigors of Aimee's evangelism schedule took a toll on the couple, and Aimee and Harold divorced in August of 1921.

In addition to her ordination by Durham, Aimee was ordained briefly as an evangelist by the Assemblies of God. Because of her popularity organizations sought to ordain her, and in the 1920s Aimee received ministerial credentials from the C. C. Hancock Memorial Church of the Methodist Episcopal Church, and the First Baptist Church of San Jose, California. Unlike many Pentecostal contemporaries, Aimee had an interdenominational outlook on ministry and was thus open to these ordinations.

The Lord's leading would bring McPherson to Los Angeles, which became the hub of her ministry for the rest of her life. In 1921 she envisioned a facility of her own in which to preach, and work began on the design and construction of the Angelus Temple. The next two years were spent preaching coast to coast and raising funds for this project. On January 1, 1923, the 5,300-seat Angelus Temple was dedicated and the International Church of the Foursquare Gospel was born. The denomination, named for its emphasis on the "Foursquare Gospel" of Jesus Christ—as Savior, Baptizer in the Holy Spirit, Healer, and Coming King—was formally incorporated four years later in December, 1927.

The Lighthouse of International Foursquare Evangelism (LIFE) Bible college was also founded in 1923. Its mission was to train pastors, evangelists, and missionaries. The following year Aimee became the first woman in the United States to receive an FCC license to operate a radio station—KFSG. Her early training in music paid dividends in this endeavor as Aimee published the *Foursquare Hymnal*, which included sixty-four of her own compositions as well as those of other Pentecostals.

Aimee always had a flare for the dramatic as she preached, drawing on her Salvation Army background and the illustrated sermons that were part of that experience. She lived a full and controversial life as a gifted missionary, preacher, publisher, radio evangelist, and founder. It is significant to note that along with the Bible college she founded, the denomination she founded now supports almost sixty Bible schools worldwide.[7]

Her life also included some troubling episodes, including a "kidnapping" in 1926, which produced as many questions about her integrity as concerns about her well being.[8][9] She had a somewhat enigmatical relationship with the Ku Klux Klan, sharing the group's patriotism but disavowing its racist policies. She also accepted the organization's support and contributions,[10] especially during the legal proceedings that followed her kidnapping. The rise in her celebrity status among Angelus Temple attendees from the Hollywood film community led to her own brief flirtation with the cinematic world.[11] In 1931 she entered into her third marriage, an ill-fated one to David L. Hutton. Ultimately, Aimee's focus would always return to her ministry.

On October 27, 1944, Aimee died of a probable overdose of sedatives in the Lemington Hotel in Oakland, California. In an auditorium nearby, Bebe Harrison Patten, a 1933 graduate of LIFE Bible College, was in the midst of the second revival series in the Bay Area, home to what would become her own ministerial and education endeavors . . . the protégé continuing the legacy of the founder lovingly known as "Sister Aimee."

---

7. Robeck, "International Church of the Foursquare Gospel," 794.
8. Robeck, "Aimee Semple McPherson," 857.
9. Alexander, *Limited Liberty*, 104.
10. Sutton, *Aimee Semple McPherson*, 115–16.
11. Ibid., 154–55.

21

Operating by the Faith Principle

Christine Amelia Gibson

Who would take care of the recently orphaned Christine Eckman and her sister Alice? Born on born January 3, 1879, in Georgetown, British Guiana (presently Guyana), to a Swedish sea captain and his South American wife, these two girls lost their parents in early childhood. Alice would initially be cared for by their grandmother and then later by relatives. Christine, however, grew up in the home of one of her mother's friends, a Scottish woman who ran a private school.

Although Christine attended the local Presbyterian church with her guardian, she did not know the Lord. She excelled in school, and one day the headmistress of the school asked her grandmother if Christine could be sent to Scotland to continue her studies. Her grandmother refused because she didn't want to send the young girl so far away.

Upon reaching adulthood, Christine went to work in the government's telephone and telegraph offices. One day after work, one of her friends invited her to visit a Salvation Army (SA) officer who was quite ill. After being introduced, Christine was increasingly restless as that evening she was to attend a ballroom dance. When queried by the SA officer about her seeming nervousness, she told him about her night's plans. He replied, "A little dance, a little hell; a little dance, a little hell." Highly offended, Christine later told her friend that she never wanted to visit that "rude man" again.

Something must have been stirred in Christine's heart, because a few days later she was walking by a Catholic church on her way home from work and felt compelled to go in. Once inside, she walked directly to the altar where others were praying and also knelt in prayer. With eyes closed, she could see the crucified Christ and she heard the words, "Do you see that man on the Cross? He took the sinner's place. He became sin for a lost world. You are a sinner. He died in your stead. You can have His righteousness, for He is your salvation."[1] In response, Christine gave her heart to the Lord.

Christine immediately shared her experience with her sister Alice and suggested that they go to the Salvation Army barracks to attend a meeting. At the close of the service, Christine went forward to pray at the mourner's bench (in the Methodist and Holiness traditions this was a bench where penitents knelt in prayer to seek salvation—later replaced by the altar call) and was soon joined by Alice. That night both girls made public confession that they had received Jesus as their personal Savior. Christine and Alice soon joined a Holiness group at the Full Gospel Mission in Georgetown and were baptized in water.

During this time, Christine met Rev. Reuben Gibson, a Christian Missionary Alliance missionary who preached occasionally at the mission. Gibson was respected for his godly life and ministry among the young people in the mission. Unfortunately, his wife had left him some time prior to meeting the Eckman sisters, and he soon afterward returned to America with his five children. The life paths of Christine and Reuben would again meet in the United States.

Conversion certainly influenced Christine's life. She was able to exhibit more self-control when she was irritated by others. She also felt a responsibility to be more accountable in taking care of her debts. In seeking to become more financially responsible, she experienced God's provision in response to her prayer of faith that He would provide for her finances. Just as God had promised, Christine was able to sell her concertina just in time to meet the due date of the payment that would clear her largest debt. This was the beginning of the "faith principle" that would be central to Christine's ministry and educational endeavors.

In 1902, there was a need to replace a missionary working in the deep jungles of the Essequibo River, ministering to South American Indians. The call went out for a man to replace him, but no one came forward except Christine. Initially, her pastor would not hear of sending a young

---

1. Mary Wilson, *Obedience of Faith*, 3.

woman to minister in such rugged conditions alone. However, after a second call for a replacement was made and only Christine volunteered, he conceded, saying, "Well, no one else has offered and you seem to have a definite calling. You may go."

Once in the jungle she lived in a small hut with a mud floor. She ministered to the Indians of the area and the Europeans who had ventured there, including a Portuguese family who operated a store in the interior. One of her converts, Mrs. Deswitt, took Christine into her home to live so that she would have better living conditions. Christine continued to minister until she became sick with malaria.

At first she did not want to inform the missionary headquarters of her illness, fearing that she would be removed from the mission field. However, her condition deteriorated to the point that she was near death. Headquarters were contacted and Christine made the trip downriver by dugout canoe to the steamer that would return her to Georgetown.

Once back at the mission she slowly recovered, and it was two weeks before she could walk. During her recovery, she became friends with an American missionary woman who suggested that Christine travel to America with her, as the American was about to return home to California. Although she believed God was leading her to make this trip, her departure was accompanied by mixed emotions.

Christine would be leaving behind her sister Alice and her many Christian friends. She had also just received a letter from Rev. Gibson, who was traveling with fellow missionaries and would soon arrive at the mission where she was. He looked forward to seeing her again and "would have much to say to her." She was less than enthusiastic about seeing this man again, given the circumstances of the breakup of his marriage (Reuben's wife left him to become a prostitute). So, she boarded the ship and journeyed to the United States.

However, upon arriving in New York in 1904, she kept thinking about Rev. Gibson, who was supposed to have set sail for British Guiana at the same time she left for America. Sensing that he was still in the country, she sent him a telegram asking him to visit. He was there the next day, and after a few words of conversation Reuben asked Christine to marry him. She refused.

Still friends, before Reuben returned to the mission field for two years he introduced Christine to Mr. and Mrs. Thomas Crocker, who were in charge of a "faith home" in East Providence, Rhode Island. Faith homes were hospices operated on a faith basis for the sick and terminally ill. Traditionally they were operated without solicitation of funds. The first American faith home was established by Carrie Judd Montgomery in 1882 in Buffalo, New York. The ministry of faith homes spanned the healing, Holiness, and Pentecostal movements. A. B. Simpson opened the Home for Faith and Physical Healing in New York City. The following year John Alexander Dowie opened Divine Healing Home Number One in Chicago, and in 1898 Charles Parham opened Bethel Healing Home in Topeka, Kansas.

Two years before Christine was born, Rev. Alpheus Angel Cleveland founded a Holiness church, simply named "Faith Church," in East Providence. By the time Christine arrived in this city, Rev. Cleveland was elderly, and he and his wife were still residents of the faith home after having turned over its management to Rev. Crocker. Continuing to serve as pastor of the church, now renamed the Church of the First Born, Rev. Cleveland was praying for a successor to replace him, and soon Christine was called to serve as the pastor in 1908.

The year 1910 was especially eventful for Christine. First, after many proposals, she married Reuben. Later, faith home resident Emma Knowlton talked to her about the Pentecostal experience. Both Christine and her congregation were resistant to this new teaching because they believed sanctification to be the second and final blessing in spiritual growth. Once convinced that God was in the experience, Christine visited the Rochester Bible Training School,[2] founded by Elizabeth Baker and her sisters, and after a time of prayer Christine experienced the baptism of the Holy Spirit.

For Christine, God came first. A year after they were married she left Reuben—and the four children living at home—because he would not quit his secular job and go into the ministry (he was resistant to living by the "faith principle") and because their children were not living good Christian lives. After a time of separation, Reuben asked for forgiveness and the couple reconciled. In 1913, when Reuben and Christine were put in charge of the faith home, the first thing that Christine did was transition out residents who were there because it was affordable housing and not because it was an opportunity for spiritual growth.

---

2. Ibid., 55.

In response to a request from a group in Windsor, Vermont, Christine traveled there to hold a series of revival meetings. Because of the great response in the services, the revival was extended. However, one day Reuben showed up "to take his wife home." The irony of the situation was that if the roles had been reversed, it would have been thought improper for her to travel to his preaching destination to bring "her husband home." Ultimately, he stayed in the city for a while and ministered alongside Christine.

The year 1924 began with great hope. Plans were being finalized for the opening of a Bible school. Christian artist Mr. Nordlen of Windsor, Vermont, was commissioned to paint a mural on the front wall of the Church of the First Born. Tragically, the first service to be held in the church after the mural was completed was the funeral for Rev. Reuben Gibson.

The year, however, ended in victory as the Mount Zion Bible School (MZBS) opened on November 24 with a beginning class of three students. The school operated on the faith principle—"no charges of any kind were placed on the students. They came, and everyone trusted God to supply the needs of Zion."[3] MZBS was renamed the School of the Prophets in its second year, and then renamed Zion Bible Institute in 1941. In 1935 Christine founded the Zion Evangelistic Fellowship, a loosely knit organization that "brought together independent churches in at least half a dozen northeastern states" serving "as an agency for life service of graduates from Zion Bible Institute."[4] Zion operated independent of denominational ties until it joined the Assemblies of God in 2000. In 2008, the school moved to a new campus, formerly the home of Bradford College, in Haverhill, Massachusetts. To this day the school offers one degree in one major—a BA in Bible.

On May 29, 1955, the day before graduation at Zion Bible Institute, Christine went home to be with the Lord. The "faith principle" had been foundation to her ministry and to how the institutions she founded—church, Bible school, children's home, *Faith* journal, radio ministry—were operated. By leaving behind an example of what trusting in God could accomplish, she ensured that the "ship of Zion," the Bible college she founded, would always travel to new horizons.

---

3. Ibid., 111.
4. Jones, "Zion Evangelistic Fellowship," 1226.

22

Affirming Indigenous Leadership . . . Almost

ALICE LUCE

ALICE LUCE (1873–1955) was born into an Episcopal home in Cheltenham, England. Her father, Rev. J. J. Luce, was the vicar of St. Nicholas Episcopal Church in Glouscester. The Luce family originally fled from France to England due to the persecution against the Huguenots, whose beliefs her family followed.

Having experienced salvation at the age of ten, she had a strong inclination toward Christian ministry. After high school, she attended the Cheltenham Ladies College,[1] then studied to become a nurse and finally pursued theological studies at the London Bible School.[2] It was in England that she first began training young people for ministry.

Under the auspices of the Church Missionary Society (CMS), Luce began to fulfill her call to ministry by traveling to India as a missionary. In Azimgarh, United Provinces, she taught at a school and ministered to women isolated in harems.

In 1910 Alice learned of the Pentecostal movement through reading a newsletter about the Azusa Street Revival and the baptism in the Holy Spirit. She then heard of two women in a certain Indian town who had been Spirit-filled. Having been convinced of the veracity of the experience, she prayed until she also received the baptism of the Holy Spirit.

During the course of her missionary work, she and a coworker became seriously ill from drinking contaminated water. Her coworker died,

1. McGee, "Alice Eveline Luce," 844.
2. De Leon, *Silent Pentecostals*, 20.

but Alice was able to recuperate enough to return home to England in 1912. The following year she was on loan from the CMS to serve as a secretary with the Zenana Bible and Medical Mission (currently the Bible and Medical Missionary Fellowship). This work required her to move to Canada, and in 1914 Alice resigned from the CMS for medical reasons.

While in Canada Alice felt that God was calling her to serve as a missionary in Mexico. The Mexican Revolution, however, at first prevented her from going there, so she traveled to Texas where she became acquainted with Sunshine Louise Marshall, Henry C. Ball, Mack M. Pinson, and Lloyd Baker. This association led to her ordination in 1915 by the General Council of the Assemblies of God, a newly formed Pentecostal organization.

Two years later Alice and Sunshine left for Monterrey, Mexico, as missionaries. However, because the Mexican Revolution made life difficult, "especially for gringos," they returned to San Antonio, Texas. Sunshine married Henry C. Ball, and Alice traveled to Los Angeles where she engaged in personal evangelism among the Spanish-speaking peoples there. In 1918 she rented a hall in the Placita (now Olvera Street) and began holding churches services.

Two years later Alice returned to England, and while in the city of Gales she met Ralph and Richard Williams. She told them of her work among the Mexicans in California and of her hope that they would become missionaries to Latin America. The Williams brothers responded that they too would soon be traveling to California, in order to attend the Glad Tidings Bible Institute (now Bethany University).

Alice continued her work and soon became convinced that best way to evangelize the Latino population would be through training evangelists and pastors in a Bible school. An immediate concern was curriculum. "When the idea of starting Bible institutes came up, Miss Luce thought that it would be a good thing for her to write Pentecostal textbooks for the schools in Spanish, because good Spanish Pentecostal literature was not to be found anywhere. The Methodist, Baptist and Presbyterian seminaries were well established in Los Angeles by 1918–20 among Hispanics, but there were no schools for the Pentecostals."[3]

Soon property was purchased at 343 17th Street in San Diego, California, for $3,000. At the time of the purchase Alice only had $250

---

3. Ibid., 64–65.

for the down payment, but trusted that the Lord would provide for the monthly payments. With Isaiah 60:22 ("A little one shall become a thousand, and a small one a strong nation: I the Lord will hasten it in his time") as assurance that God would provide, the Berean Bible Institute was born in 1926.

Ralph Williams, whom Alice had met during her most recent trip to England, became the first superintendent of the school. Ralph and his wife would later move to Mexico to teach at a Bible school there, after which his brother Richard served as Berean's second superintendent. Beyond her missionary zeal, Alice impressed the Williams brothers with her proficiency in five languages—English, French, Hindu, Urdu, and Spanish.

The school would experience two relocations in Southern California, first to Mesa in 1935 and then to Belvedere in 1941, before being established in its permanent home in La Puente. Its name was also changed to the Latin American Bible Institute.

The initial two-year course of study included courses in Personal evangelism, Christian doctrine, prophecy, types of Christ, music, rhetoric, Bible geography, synthetic studies in the Old and New Testaments, divine healing, types of the Holy Spirit, Christian evidence, homiletics, and pastoral theology. The first graduating class in 1928 consisted of D. Adeline Sugg, Ursula Riggio, and Maria Grajeda.

The legacy of Luce's work among Latinos of the Southwest, however, would be threefold. The first was the Latin American Bible Institute, as it both pioneered the missions work of the Assemblies of God among Latinos and, more importantly, played a crucial role in the formation of Latino Pentecostal identity. "Bible institutes were part of the pedagogy of orthodoxy that LABI began during the Assemblies of God's second decade of existence, when debates about the need for formalized education plagued the Euro American branch, education was viewed as an essential component of creating and maintaining a Latino Pentecostal identity."[4]

Motivated by a premillennial perspective, Luce's initial evangelistic work involved taking the message of the gospel to a predominately Catholic Latino population. As converts were added to the fold and churches were established, she then sought ways to expand this evangelistic work and to establish new believers in the faith.

---

4. Sénchez Walsh, *Latino Pentecostal Identity*, 49.

At the same time, her efforts as a Pentecostal were challenged by the "New Issue" involving a reformation of the water baptism formula, and the Oneness doctrine, which had recently emerged. The challenges Alice faced included establishing and maintaining orthodoxy within the churches being established while allowing Latino Pentecostals to achieve their own unique blend of religious beliefs, ethnic values, traditions, and practices.

Alice's work prepared "preachers to learn the Bible, trust the Spirit, and guard against doctrinal errors and, in doing so, lead exemplary lives for others to emulate. LABI became a training ground for Latino ministers because, Luce, the missionary and teacher, helped lead the first generation to their reality, not as Catholic converts, but as Pentecostals."[5]

The second major component of Alice's legacy was in the curriculum she developed for ministerial training at LABI, and her prolific writing for Assemblies of God publications. During LABI's first twenty years, Alice wrote most of the books and notes that made up the school's curriculum, which was also used by other Latin American Bible institutes. She wrote several books, published by the Gospel Publishing House: *El Mensajero y Su Mensaje: Manual para Obreros Cristianos* ("The Messenger and His Message: A Manual for Christian Workers," 1925), *The Little Flock in the Last Days* (1927), *Pictures of Pentecost* (n.d.), *Estudios de las Evidencias Cristianas* ("Studies in Christian Evidence"), and *Hermeneutica: Introduccion Biblica* ("Hermeneutics: Bible Introduction"). Alice was a regular contributor to *Apostolic Light*, which was published by Henry C. Ball, and she wrote "lesson components for intermediate and senior Sunday School teachers' quarterlies for many years."[6]

Alice was also a pioneer in producing and translating literature among Latino Pentecostals. Rev. Teresa Ruelas, a retired Asambleas de Dios minister, recalled her encounter with literature produced by "Miss Luce" in the fall of 1946. Having migrated from Mexico to the United States, the country of her birth, Teresa was setting up her living quarters in the basement of her uncle Rev. Antonio Muela's home in Alvarado, California. During these preparations she came across a box that had been mailed to the home by Alice Luce. Inside she found Bible lessons and simple projects for vacation Bible school. That encounter led to Teresa's

---

5. Ibid., 59.
6. McGee, G. H., "Alice Eveline Luce," 845.

twenty-five-year ministry in vacation Bible school and thirty years as a Missionette leader in several Asambleas de Dios churches.

The third facet of the legacy of Alice Luce would be the "articulation of a missionary strategy for the Assemblies of God."[7] Her missionary work among these people was distinct because Alice veered away from the colonialist perspective that framed many missionary approaches. Instead of mistrusting indigenous leadership, she embraced developing indigenous leaders and handing over leadership to them. In this Alice Luce was a pioneer.[8]

According to her, "it seems to me that we have a fundamental principle which we do well to observe, namely that of handing over the oversight of everything that concerns the local church to its own members . . . The native Christian would make mistakes but they would learn from their failures, as we all do; and if only we could keep humble enough to help and advise them when they ask us to do so and to eliminate ourselves to submit ourselves to them whenever possible, we could teach them to walk alone."[9]

Where she fell short of this ideal was in attempting to maintain the Trinitarian orthodoxy among her congregants. Her solution for keeping the Mexicans in line was to send more Anglo missionaries. "This will result in keeping them [Mexican assemblies] from many of the specious errors which are being spread in such a subtle way among the Spanish-speaking people in this day. In many places the New Issue and other false teachers have become strongly entrenched among them in the years gone by because there was no American Assembly to watch over the Spanish one and warn it of its error."[10]

Despite this one area of reservation, Alice succeeded in establishing "self-supporting, self-governing and self-propagating New Testament churches."[11] According to Victor DeLeon, Alice "will always be remembered as the tutor of many of the Spanish-speaking ministers in the early beginnings of Pentecostalism, especially among the Latin American Assemblies of God. Alice E. Luce became synonymous with Latin American people, the Bible Institute and God."[12]

7. Ibid., 844.
8. Wilson and Wilson, "Alice E. Luce," 169.
9. Luce, "Scriptural Methods," 8–9.
10. Luce, "Latin American Pentecostal Work," 7.
11. McGee, "Alice Eveline Luce," 845.
12. De Leon, *Silent Pentecostals*, 64–65.

23

Fulfilling the Vision of the Founder

Mary Keith

AFRICAN AMERICAN WOMEN EMERGED from the American slavery experience in the United States echoing the words of Sojourner Truth spoken at the 1851 women's rights convention in Akron, Ohio: "I have born thirteen chilern and seen em mos' all sold off into slavery, and when I cried out with a mother's grief, none but Jesus heard—and ar'n't I a woman."[1]

Although spoken ten years before the Civil War, these words still resonated with African American women in the post-Emancipation era. The struggle to establish their place in American society was shaped by both the racist culture in which they lived and influenced by the emasculation experiences—social, economic, emotional, and physical—of their black male counterparts during and after slavery. While in the post-slavery era black males were given some rights and opportunities because they were men, that progress was impeded because they were black. One arena in which there was a significant impact was the black church, both then and now. "Hence, the roadblocks to preaching for black women were further compounded by the complex problem of black male identity in a racist society. If the ministry was the only route to even a shadow of masculinity, the inclusion of women seemed very much like a gratuitous defeat for everybody."[2]

---

1. White, *Ar'n't I a Woman?*, 14.
2. Lincoln and Mamiya, *Black Church*, 278.

Fulfilling the Vision of the Founder

As was true for their white female counterparts, black females became the core constituents and backbone of their churches and denominations. An equal reality was exclusion of women from ministerial and leadership roles within these religious bodies. However, within the black community, there seemed to be a communal defense mechanism in which black women acquiesced in the area of gender rights to preserve a sense of self-respect within, and the respect of others for, the black males in their lives. "Many women preferred to remain in the background while nudging—sometimes rather forcefully—their husbands, brothers, fathers, ministers, and sons into the forefront of leadership. However, there are always a small number of women in whom the spark of leadership was too great to be so easily quenched."[3] One such woman was Mary Magdalena. Born halfway through Reconstruction on January 5, 1871, to John and Mary Street, she was able to carve out a significant place in American religious history.

In 1890, Mary Magdalena began her faith journey as a member of the Methodist Church, and at age nineteen she experienced conversion and a call to preach. She also married David Lewis, her first husband (she would marry four times in her lifetime), who was also a Methodist. Their sons, Walter Curtis and Felix Early, were born in Vanlier, Tennessee. Mary Magdalena would eventually leave the Methodist Church because of disagreements over certain church practices and the church's position against women preachers.

According to some scholars it was during this time period in her life that Mary Magdalena was affiliated with the Church of the Living God (Christian Workers for Fellowship), which was established by William Christian.[4] This is significant because when Mary Magdalena formed her own group she would insist that the name of her denomination and the practice of using water and unleavened bread during the sacrament of communion came directly from God. However, both the name "Church of the Living God" and the unique communion practice were part of Christian's ministry.

In 1903 Mary Magdalena began her public ministry, which included door-to-door evangelism, street preaching, and home Bible studies in her community. One casualty of her ministry was her marriage to

---

3. Lewis, *Mary Lena Lewis Tate: Vision!*, 3.
4. Alexander, *Limited Liberty*, 63.

David. They divorced because of his objection to her street ministry and the amount of time it took her away from their family. Ironically David and his new family would later become active members of his ex-wife's church, and he and Mary Magdalena would be lifelong friends. In that same year, Mary Magdalena established her first church, the Latter Day Saints of the Foundation of True Holiness and Sanctification, an independent Holiness church.

For the next five years, Mary Magdalena expanded the geographic scope of her ministry, traveling on "what her followers were later to term 'missionary journeys,' to such cities as Brooklyn, Illinois; Paducah, Kentucky; St. Louis, Missouri, Paris, Tennessee; and Montgomery, Alabama."[5] Her message was one of "true holiness" and in each city she borrowed churches to hold her revival services, and from those in attendance she established "holiness bands" and "do-right bands." Although she was establishing a network of believers, she made no attempt at this time to bring about organizational structure to these groups.

In other parts of the country the Pentecostal revival had begun, first at Parham's Bethel Bible School and later at the Azusa Street Revival beginning in 1906. Mary Magdalena's own Pentecostal experience occurred as the result of a near fatal illness she suffered in 1908. Although she was not expected to live, she was miraculously healed. Her healing was accompanied by Spirit baptism with speaking in tongues as evidence of that baptism. Her second task after sharing her experience with leaders and members of her church was to convince them that she was not mentally ill. She succeeded, and many in her church also experienced Spirit baptism. To the church's doctrines of holiness and sanctification was added the doctrine of the baptism of the Holy Spirit with initial evidence of speaking in tongues.

A revival later that year in Greenville, Alabama, became the foundation from which Mary Magdalena would form the Church of the Living God the Pillar and Ground of the Truth (CLGPGT). Her denomination's board of trustees ordained Mary Magdalena a bishop, and she was named First Chief Overseer of the group. With these two actions, Mary Magdalena became the first woman in United States history to hold the rank of bishop in a national Christian body, and one of the first women to serve as presiding presbyters of a Protestant Christian denomination.

5. Ibid.

Fulfilling the Vision of the Founder

Mary Magdalena's goal was to restore the church to its New Testament foundations and practices. Her vision for the denomination included developing "institutions and . . . educational facilities for the Church, Bible training schools and business colleges, general and local orphanages and rescue homes, academies, local schools . . . facilities along educational lines necessary for the church . . ."[6] Although she would leave behind a well-established and organized denomination and found an academy, the fulfillment of others parts of her vision would be accomplished by one of her successors, Mary Frankie Giles Lewis Keith.

Mary Frankie was born the second child of George Meadows and Flora "Fannie" Giles in 1888. Her sisters and brothers were Berta, Lillie Mae, Pearl, Elmer, George, and Robert. Raised in the state of Georgia, Mary completed eighth grade, "becoming, what historically was referred to as, 'an eighth-grade scholar,' which enabled her to teach in the elementary grades."[7]

Mary Frankie's family became part of the Mary Lena's CLGPGT during its early years in Georgia. Not only did they embrace the church's doctrines of holiness and sanctification, but a number experienced the baptism of the Holy Ghost. Ultimately Mary Frankie and her brother George Fred would rise in the ecclesiastical ranks of the church.

While living in Lumpkin, Georgia, with her family, Mary Frankie met Walter Curtis Lewis, the son of Mary Lena, and they eventually married. The new couple then moved to Waycross to live near Walter's mother and the rest of the family. In 1914, Walter was ordained to the state bishopric with the CLGPGT. Mary Frankie became indispensable to her husband's ministry. She served as his personal secretary, ministered to congregants, and preached in his pulpit while Walter was away on church matters. She also taught part-time when the family struggled financially. For his part, Walter worked in the coal mines when his ministry took them to the state of Pennsylvania. Between 1913 and 1921 six children were born to the couple: Robert David, Pearlana, Walter Curtis Jr., Israel Paul, Felix Early III, and Mary Curtese ("Sydnie"). Unfortunately, Walter Sr. died on February 7, 1921, just six months before the birth of Sydnie.

Mary Frankie's role within her mother-in-law's church now began to change dramatically. In addition to being a seasoned preacher, she had

---

6. Ibid., 69.
7. Lewis, *Mary Lena Lewis Tate: A Street Called Straight*, 29.

demonstrated her acumen in organization, bookkeeping, and writing. She was also known as an "influencer" of others' thinking. Mary Frankie was soon appointed to fill the administrative role previously held by her husband. Her area of responsibility stretched from Connecticut to Georgia and into Florida. As she had been working with the elders and bishops in this area as part of her ministry with her husband, they easily accepted her leadership role. In the late 1920s, Mary Frankie married Lonnie Keith.[8]

On December 28, 1930, Mary Magdalena Lewis Tate went home to be with the Lord. The following year, the CLGPGT Supreme Executive Council decided against passing on the leadership of the denomination to one individual. Instead, the council created a "triumvirate," with Felix Early Lewis, Bruce Lee McLeod, and Mary Frankie ordained as Chief Overseers. Together with the elders and bishops in her "Dominion," the denomination expanded its presence in Connecticut, Delaware, Indiana, Kentucky, Maryland, Michigan, New York, North and South Carolina, Ohio, Pennsylvania, and Virginia. During this time period she married Lonnie Keith, and the "Keith Dominion" (as it is known today) chose as its name, The House of God which is The Church of the Living God, the Pillar and Ground of Truth without Controversy, Inc. (Later in its history the name was unofficially shortened to The House of God Church).

In fulfillment of the higher education and orphanage portions of founder Mary Magdalena's dream, in 1940 Mary Frankie founded the Keith Bible Institute in Ooltewah, Tennessee, and the House of God Home for Children in East Chattanooga, Tennessee. The purpose of the Institute was to train the denomination's ministers. The House of God Home was a place for ministers, church officials, and children to be healed and cured of diseases. In 1943, the Keith Bible Institute hosted a Keith Dominion Executive Supreme Council meeting that set in place many of the denominational policies and procedures for both the denomination's clergy and lay members.

In 1948 Mary Frankie built a sanctuary at the denominational headquarters in Nashville, Tennessee, as well as men's and women's dormitories. In the area of church curriculum, she was responsible for the publication of the first *Universal Sunday School Lessons*. She also financed and edited the publication of *Spiritual Songs and Hymns*, which included a number

---

8. Lewis, *Mary Lena Lewis Tate: Vision!*, 206.

of songs that Mary Magdalena likely authored,[9] and *Church Song Books*. During her administration, Mary Frankie was determined to live by the spiritual counsel she gave others: "Stay in the Faith and Doctrine."

In the area of education, Mary Frankie set high goals for herself. She earned Bachelor of Theology and Doctor of Divinity degrees from Moody Bible Institute, and later a Doctor of Letters degree. Beyond personal achievement, Mary Frankie's accomplishments in academia were motivated by a desire to effectively minister to others. "She firmly believed that the better trained one is, the better service one can give."[10] On July 14, 1962, Mary Frankie Giles Lewis Keith went home to be with the Lord, and continues to be remembered as a "great Spiritual Leader, Educator, Master Builder, a Mother and a Woman of Good Deeds."[11]

---

9. Alexander, *Limited Liberty*, 77.
10. House of God Church, "Celebrating 100 Years," 5.
11. "Bishop Mary F. L. Keith," 1.

24

Answering God's Call in the Middle of the Detroit River

Bebe Patten

Wilma Bebe Harrison was in the middle of the Detroit River in an international swimming race when something "suddenly gripped her. She felt paralyzed, almost in panic. Suddenly stricken, she couldn't move her legs or kick her feet. Her brother, Lloyd, and her two coaches watched her from the boat. 'Shall we take you out?' they asked.

'No . . . no . . . no,' she said.

Then God spoke to Bebe, 'Will you give this up? THIS IS IT! This is the last time!'

'Yes, Lord,' she said—right in the middle of the Detroit River. 'God, if You help me win, I'll give You my all. I'll never swim in competition again!'"[1]

Wilma Bebe won the race and answered God's call to ministry.

Arriving at this moment had its genesis in Wilma Bebe's early childhood. Born to Newton and Maticia Harrison on September 3, 1913, Wilma Bebe was raised in a non-religious home in Waverly, Tennessee. At elementary school she was taught by her aunt Pauline Whitson, who later joined the faculty of Cornell University.

When she was five years old, Wilma Bebe was playing on the porch of the school while her aunt corrected papers inside the classroom. From across the street came music that tugged at Wilma Bebe's heart and awak-

---

1. Kunkel, *Winning the Race*, 32.

ened a spiritual hunger that would span her lifetime. The little girl wandered across the street and into a church service.

Later in life, she remembered it as "an old-fashioned, Bible-believing, hand-clapping, foot-stomping Methodist church." She sat on a back pew and watched in wonder as the parishioners raised their arms and others walked up and down the aisles singing and praying. Wilma Bebe was mustering up the courage to imitate the people raising their arms when she felt a tap on her shoulder. It was Aunt Pauline, who quickly led her out of the church. In a few years the Harrison family would move to Detroit, but that experience in the Methodist church remained in Wilma's heart.

Faith would again walk into Wilma Bebe's life when she was ten years old. She attended a special service of the Woodard Avenue Church of Christ with her brother, sister, and some of their friends. During the altar call, with the congregation singing William Kirkatrick's hymn, "Lord, I'm Coming Home," Wilma Bebe tried to walk down the aisle but was stopped by her sister.

Undeterred, Wilma Bebe sat back down and waited for the right moment to bolt for the altar, where she gave her heart to the Lord. A few weeks later, against her parents' wishes, she was baptized in water by the pastor, Rev. Maurice West. During her baptism he declared to the congregation, "I see this child preaching to thousands of people. She will be a great evangelist. She will be a great missionary leading thousands of people to Christ." As she had never heard of a woman evangelist, the only word that made sense to her was "missionary."

During high school, her spiritual zeal waned as most of her time was consumed by school work, music, playing on the basketball team, and swimming. It was through swimming, however, that Wilma Bebe gained prominence. Talented at free-style, she soon became a long-distance swimmer, winning five- and ten-mile races.

It was through local newspaper coverage of her athletic accomplishments that she came to the attention of Matty Hinson, a member of the Detroit Full Gospel Church. Matty felt the leading of the Lord to invite Wilma Bebe to her church. Matty went to the Harrison home and made the invitation on three separate occasions before Wilma Bebe's mother agreed to let her attend.

The following Sunday the two new friends attended church, and Wilma Bebe came in contact with the Pentecostal experience for the first time.

> There were hundreds of people with hands uplifted in the Spirit—singing praises to God, oblivious to those around them. And the singing sounded like the language of another world—the language of the Spirit that only those in heaven might know.
>
> Bebe drank it all in as the power of God swept over the church. She felt a depth of love she had never known, flowing from God's people. Some were speaking in languages she had never heard. Amazed at what she saw and felt, she prayed, "O Lord, whatever this is, I want it."[2]

She soon began regularly attending this church, where Dr. Giles Knight was pastor. Seeing the call of God upon her life, Dr. Knight gave Wilma Bebe opportunities to preach, first to the young people's group and later to the congregation in regular services.

Although she was growing more fulfilled spiritually and gaining experience from her early preaching experiences, her family had another course in life for her to follow. Wilma Bebe was to attend Cornell University where her Aunt Pauline was on faculty. There she was to pursue academics, swimming, music and the arts.

All the contradictory pressures on the life of this young lady came into final conflict during that fateful race across the Detroit River. However, when Wilma Bebe said, "Yes, Lord," all the inner turmoil ceased and her life course was set.

The weekend after her decision in the Detroit River, Wilma Bebe fasted and prayed Saturday and Sunday until she received the baptism of the Holy Spirit. She then announced to her parents that she would attend Bible school, to which they responded with strong resistance. Her family would not support her education, so she would have to depend on the Lord for provision.

Although adamantly opposed to his daughter leaving home to pursue a religious career, her father inadvertently provided Wilma Bebe a way to finance the start of her venture. He got her a job as a receptionist with Dr. Wolfgang, a local Jewish pediatrician. With her earnings from that job she was able to buy a one-way ticket to Los Angeles to attend Bible school.

Dr. Wolfgang impacted Wilma Bebe in two important ways. Although at first he tried to help her reconcile her differences with her family, he finally counseled her that she should "above all things, be true to

2. Ibid., 21.

your convictions and your dreams, and God will go with you." Secondly, her long conversations with Dr. Wolfgang about their two faith traditions gave her a lifelong appreciation for Judaism and re-emphasized for her Israel's place in prophesy.

In preparation for ministry, Wilma Bebe traveled cross country to LIFE Bible College in Los Angeles. The LIFE community was introduced to "Willie Bee" Harrison (though she would go by Bebe), the aspiring girl preacher from Detroit. As a student, Willie Bee set a pattern that would be a template for her life's ministry: preaching, leading song services, working on the school paper, radio broadcasting, and singing in the Hallelujah Choir and the Gold Link Trio.

Bebe graduated from LIFE in 1933, the same year she was licensed to preach by the Foursquare Church. In 1934 she became an ordained Foursquare minister, and after two years of evangelistic work Bebe was re-ordained in 1935 by the Interdenominational Ministerial Association of Evangelism.

Advertising herself as the "Girl Evangelist," Bebe evangelized in the South with Mabel Lawsen, a fellow graduate of LIFE. They worked harmoniously together until each felt a call to a specific part of the United States—Bebe to the South and Mabel to the North. They parted ways and Bebe commenced in earnest her evangelist work in the Southern states.

While ministering in the South, Bebe met her future husband, Carl Thomas Patten. Bebe was hesitant to marry because she saw so many of her female classmates at LIFE give up their ministerial aspirations when they married. After Carl convinced her that he was committed to "back a woman preacher," they married. A successful ministry together followed in which Carl supported Bebe's work in evangelism, revivals, faith healing, radio ministry, publications, song writing, and serving as pastor.

Their journey ultimately led in 1944 to Oakland, California, where Bebe held a nineteen-week revival. At the end of the revival, she gave a call to ministry to which several hundred people responded.

As there was no Bible school locally for the converts to attend, Bebe founded the Oakland Bible Institute. Many of the first students were men returning from military service in World War II who had not finished high school. The Academy of Christian Education was thus founded to enable them to finish high school. A revival center attached to the institute was organized into Christian Temple, the campus church.

Persecution, however, was to mark the Patten's early years in Oakland. In 1949, the parsonage they lived in suffered heavy damage in a fire thought to be deliberately set.[3] The following year, Carl was convicted of defrauding members of the ministry of $14,750.[4] His sentence was five to fifty years, of which he served three[5] years at San Quentin and Soledad. Most of the prosecution's testimony came from disgruntled former members of Christian Temple. During the trial Carl suffered a heart attack that temporarily moved court proceedings to the chapel of the hospital where he was being treated. In prison, Carl would suffer two more heart attacks. The main condition of his parole was that he not participate in any fundraising or promotion activities of Bebe's ministry. Carl's health deteriorated and he went home to be with the Lord on Mother's Day, May 11, 1958. A year after Carl's home-going, Bebe married John Roberto, an assistant minister in the church and 18 years her junior. This marriage was ill-fated and short-lived, ending after a couple years when it was annulled.

The ministry retrenched and began rebuilding in a new facility and location. The embattlement experience that was part of the trial impacted the campus community psyche for decades to come. To ensure that never in the future would the financial integrity of her ministries be called into question, stringent financial controls were put into place.

Undaunted by scandal and setbacks, Bebe determined even more strongly to stay faithful to God regardless of how dark the cloud of persecution that had overshadowed her ministry and that of Carl, her faithful co-laborer. Today Patten University, Patten Academy of Christian Education and Christian Cathedral, the ministries which she founded in those early years in Oakland, are a testimony to that faithfulness.

Preaching until six months before her homegoing, Bebe passed away on January 25, 2004, at the age of ninety.

3. "Mystery Fire Hits Bebe Patten Home."
4. "Patten Trial Is Ordered to Move."
5. "No More Church Fund Work."

25

That They May Reach Their Own Tribes in the Native Language

Alta Washburn

Alta Washburn's ministry to the Native Americans of the Southwest began in 1931 as she lay in bed dying of scarlet fever. Her aunt had recently been saved at a service held by an itinerant preacher in a gospel tent.

This preacher, a World War I veteran, felt that the Lord had spared his life in wartime, so he committed his life to spreading the gospel. This life-sparing work of God would soon be visited on Alta. Her newly saved Aunt Elva worked tirelessly in caring for her niece and witnessed to her of God's saving grace.

A resistant Alta then had a vision that indicated what would happen if she did not accept Christ's salvation. "Sometime after midnight I went into the jaws of death. I was suspended over the abyss of hell on a narrow slippery path struggling to climb and escape the creatures who reached to drag me."[1]

She gave her heart to the Lord and was immediately healed. Alta's decision-making process was aided in part by the all-night prayer vigil held for her by her aunt's church in Fairmont, West Virginia. Regarding the significance of this experience Alta wrote, "what a day to be remembered when I arose from the bed that had long held me prisoner. More glorious was my deliverance from the bondage of sin. Not only does that day in 1931 mark the date of my salvation and healing, but it was the day

---

1. Washburn, undated correspondence.

I heard God call me to be a missionary. Little did I know what the future held for me."[2]

Alta walked into that future slowly, first serving as a youth leader and then as a tent evangelist who brought many souls to Christ. She then served as pastor of the First Assembly church in Salinville, Ohio. She was later influenced by the dedication of the Beadles, a couple who served as missionaries to the Native Americans. The Beadles, along with Ernest and Ethel Marshall, had been sent out from the Assemblies of God (AG) church in Salineville, Ohio, where Alta served as pastor. The Beadles established the first AG church among the San Carlos Apache Natives in Arizona.

Alta then felt her own call to the Native Americans. "With this commission from the Lord, an intense love for American Indians flooded my soul. Now that I had a confirmation of my call from God, I knew I must take the next step—the step of faith."[3]

Alta became a missionary at a time in the history of missionary work in which she could effect a role reversal and also have an impact on the missiology of the Assemblies of God. She greatly benefited from the egalitarian spirit of Pentecostals, who saw both women and men as equally empowered by the Holy Spirit to spread the gospel and minister to the sick and dying.

Within the American context, the first role of women in the mission field was to serve as missionary wives. "The first American women to serve as foreign missionaries in 1812 were among the best-educated women of their time. Although barred from obtaining a college education or ministerial credentials like their husbands, the early missionary wives read their Jonathan Edwards and Samuel Hopkins."[4] While sharing their husbands' goal of spreading the gospel, their focus tended to be on their own "usefulness, concern for women and children, and the necessity of serving their husbands."[5]

During the late nineteenth century, the majority of the cadre of women serving as missionaries consisted of single women, working under the slogan of "Woman's Work for Woman." Building on the previous

---

2. Washburn, *Trail to the Tribes*, 4–5.
3. Ibid., 13.
4. Robert, *American Women in Mission*, xvii.
5. Ibid., 37.

work of missionary wives, this later group of women centered their work on educational efforts, medical care, and evangelism—ironically, this included ministry to men, even though the intent was for women to win other women to Christ. However, women now outnumbered men in missions work, and their focus on benevolence ministry had a transformative effect on American missions. Entering the mission field during the twentieth century, Alta's marriage was an example of role reversal in mission service. Her husband Clarence provided financial support for their household and Alta's ministerial efforts, living counter to the established missionary paradigm in that he was the "missionary's husband."

In being a part of Pentecostalism and, more particularly, the Assemblies of God, Alta benefited from the early egalitarian attitude of both movements. A. J. Tomlinson, the first general overseer of the Church of God, Cleveland, reflected this attitude of gender equality within early Pentecostalism in this published prayer:

> O, God, give us an army of men and women who will fear nothing but God. Set them on fire with such holy zeal that no cries of fanaticism, delusion of the devil, manifestation of the flesh, or anything else will check the fervor or impede the progress until this glorious gospel is heralded to the uttermost parts of the earth and the full blaze of Pentecostal power, with its signs, wonders and divers miracles and gifts of the Holy Ghost are ablaze and utilized for the glory of God, as at the beginning of the glorious gospel Age.[6]

The Assemblies of God seemed to glory in embracing this equal call and empowering of women and men for ministry, as reflected in a 1915 issue of the denominational magazine *Evangel*:

> We know of no Movement where women of ability and filled with the Holy Ghost have been more highly honored or given much more freedom than among us. She is given the right to be ordained, to preach, witness, give advice, act as evangelist, missionary, etc. The only thing not thrown unscripturally on her weak shoulders is making of her a Ruler Elder ... Even her we allow such liberty as not to interfere [sic] with special calls God in His sovereignty may give to women under exceptional circumstances.[7]

---

6. Tomlinson, "Better Obey God Than Listen to Man," 1.
7. Tucker and Liefeld, *Daughters of the Church*, 364.

Indeed, during the early part of the twentieth century, the Assemblies of God denomination was exceptional in the ministerial opportunities it provided women.[8]

Having served as a senior pastor, Alta entered missions work to Native Americans in which these indigenous believers had already taken initial steps to claim and form their own identity as Pentecostal Native Americans. By embracing the self-empowering steps of Native American believers and acting on her belief in developing indigenous leadership, Alta was able to impact the previous model of paternalistic missiology. She accomplished this by example, thereby moving the Assemblies of God to embrace indigenization as the optimal mode for missiology.

In 1946 Alta and Clarence began their labor in the mission field of the San Carlos Reservation in San Carlos, Arizona. Actually, the work established there was closer to a vibrant Pentecostal church in its early beginnings, the result of diligent ministry by the Beadles and the Marshalls. Alta was also able to see firsthand a Native American preaching to his own—the Apache evangelist Dick Boni.

Experiences both violent and miraculous characterized her ministry on the reservation. On one occasion a man brandishing a gun came looking for his own wife and child during a church service. When he saw them he began beating them, and finally was restrained by two tribal police officers who charged into the building. Although injured, both mother and child soon recovered.

On another occasion, while she was ministering on an Apache reservation, one of the tribal women handed Alta the lifeless body of her child. Alta immediately sought the Lord's healing for the baby. "As I prayed, I began to feel warmth return to that little body and the rigid little limbs become limp and movable. I handed the baby restored back to life into its mother's arms. All of us in that Sunday service were overcome with the knowledge that we had actually beheld the resurrection power of the Lord."[9] Alta found support during a time of great difficulty in her ministry in San Carlos from her friendship with two missionary couples, the Beadles and Imogene and Ted Johnson (her sister and brother-in-law).

After some time, the Washburns moved to Phoenix because Clarence had difficulty finding employment on the reservation since he was an

---

8. Ibid.
9. Washburn, *Trail to the Tribes*, 22.

"Anglo." Their new venue provided Alta and Clarence opportunities to minister to tribes in the Phoenix area such as the Pima, Maricopa, Yaqui, and Papago. They started this ministry effort in collaboration with the First Assembly of God church, and then in 1948 they founded the All Tribes Assembly of God.

The church-planting efforts of the All Tribes Assembly of God resulted in churches in Laveen and Casa Blanca (Gila River Indian Reservation), a church in Guadalupe (Yaqui Indian community near Phoenix) and a Salt River Assemblies of God (Salt River Indian Reservation). Increasingly it became evident to Alta that there was a need for a ministry school to train Native Americans and equip them for leadership in their own communities. Like Alice Luce, who pioneered Assemblies of God outreach ministry to the Latinos of the Southwest, Alta believed in a missionary model that empowered indigenous people.[10] To this end, she wanted to establish a training center to develop this type of leadership.

Establishing such a school was especially important because "up to that time very few Native leaders had attended any sort of Bible college training, noteworthy among the small number who had were Charles E. Lee (Navajo), a graduate of (then) Central Bible Institute in Springfield, Missouri, and Andrew C. Maracle (Mohawk), who completed his studies at (then) Zion Bible Institute of Barrington, Rhode Island."[11]

"On September 23, 1957 the All Tribes Indian Bible Training School (ABTS) opened its doors at 4123 E. Washington Street in Phoenix, Arizona."[12] The purpose of the school was "to train the native Indian worker in sound Bible doctrines that they may in turn go out to reach their own tribes in the native language, thereby spreading the Gospel quickly to every kindred, tribe and tongue."[13]

From humble beginnings (tuition was originally $20 a year, room and board $5 a week, and beans were a main staple in meals) Alta was able to establish and grow the All Tribes Indian Bible Training School. She also successfully resisted denominational pressure to make her school a training ground for Native Americans to serve as pastoral assistants. Instead, the school operated according to Alta's intended purpose of equipping

---

10. Saggio, "Alta M. Washburn: An Iconoclastic Pentecostal 'Trailblazer,'" 2.
11. Ibid., 6.
12. Saggio, "Alta M. Washburn: 'Trailblazer,'" 31.
13. Ibid.

Native Americans for pastoral ministry and church leadership. Today the school is the only regionally accredited Bible college for Native Americans in the United States. After a couple name changes, it is now the American Indian College of the Assemblies of God.

Due to health issues, Alta stepped down from her leadership role in the school in 1965. Alta and Clarence continued as pastors of the All Tribes Assemblies of God in Phoenix until 1972. At that point, they moved to Prescott to minister among the Yavapai Apaches and then to the Native Americans on the Salt River Indian Reservation. In 1985, at the age of seventy-nine, Alta accepted her final pastorate, at the Yaqui church in Guadalupe, which she had planted while serving as pastor at All Tribes several years before.

Always seeking God's guidance in the steps she took in ministry, she believed that God was in this last assignment. "I could never close a door that God opened for me, nor could I close this one. Had I not proved many times that God's strength and grace sustained me in spite of obstacles to fulfilling His will? Yes, I could accept the pastorate."[14]

In 1990 Alta went home to be with her Lord after completing her memoirs, *Trail to the Tribes*, with the help of her friend and colleague Alma Thomas.

---

14. Washburn, *Trail to the Tribes*, 99.

26

The Mantle of God Is upon Her

Violet Kiteley

Violet Whitney was born in Vancouver, British Columbia, to Albert and Mary Jane Whitney on August 31, 1925. Born into a family of some means, her father owned quite a bit of acreage in the area. However, during the Great Depression Albert lost everything and the family suffered a life of deprivation. Violet's childhood experience would lead to a lifelong commitment to frugality in her personal finances and a generosity toward others in need.

Violet's parents were very devout members of the Holiness movement, and at age six she came to know the Lord. When she reached the age of twelve Violet was last in line to be baptized in water at the Kingsway Foursquare Church in Vancouver. As she approached Aimee Semple McPherson, the minister baptizing the converts, Violet remembers that Aimee "put her hand on my head and said that the mantle of God was on [me] and I would minister around the world."[1] As at that time there were few women in public ministry, Aimee served as an inspiration and role model for Violet to follow as she answered God's call on her life.

Violet's first involvement in ministry was assisting her father in rescue mission work and street preaching, which she began at the age of fifteen. Having experienced the financial devastation of the Great Depression, Albert became a man of faith and "prayed in everything." This faith principle he instilled in Violet. As a young adult, Violet assisted in a mission church in downtown Vancouver. When the person in charge of the mis-

---

1. Lawson, "Kiteley Family a Point of Light in Troubled Oakland," 1.

sion was drafted for military service in World War II, Violet was handed the responsibility of running the mission. As pastors of Assemblies of God churches were also being drafted, she began to teach Sunday school and preach from the pulpit.

In 1944 Violet married Raymond Valentine Kiteley, a member of the Royal Canadian Air Force. Less than one year later, on July 13, 1945, Raymond was killed at age twenty in a fiery airplane crash. At the time he had less than three months to serve, after which time the young couple had planned to go to Africa as missionaries. At the time of his death, Violet was pregnant with their son David, and after he was born Violet remained hospitalized and was unable to walk for nine months.

On November 26, 1946, a missionary from the country that was then called Transjordan was flying to Vancouver. While on the plane he received a prophetic word that there was a young woman who had lost her husband and that the missionary was not to go to his hotel until he prayed for her. The missionary prayed for Violet's paralysis and gave her the message God had directed him to deliver: she would be raised up that very day and be given a new message to preach around the world—and her son would become a prophet to carry the same message. Instantly she was healed. She then began to share her testimony in the local churches and other churches in that region.

In 1948 Violet was in prayer when an older woman came in to tell her of a new move of God that was occurring at the Sharon Orphanage and Schools in North Battleford, Saskatchewan. The Sharon organization, which included a high school, an orphanage, a technical institute, and a Bible school, was organized by Revs. George Hawtin, Ernest Hawtin, and Percy Hunt as part of an organizational schism with the Bethel Bible Institute of Saskatoon, Canada. What followed was a controversial renewal movement within Pentecostalism.

The extended chapel services held February 11–14, 1948 at the Sharon Bible School had been preceded by extended fasting periods intended to strengthen the spiritual power of students. During the chapels, individuals in attendance were called forward, and through the laying on hands and prophetic utterances they were empowered with specific gifts of the Holy Spirit. Other manifestations of the Spirit also became part of worship services, such as the "heavenly choir," in which those in attendance would sing in a heavenly language in unison. News of this revival movement spread, and as more people were attracted to these services, classes at the Bible school were suspended, and conferences and camp meetings replaced religious training.

The timing of this renewal movement coincided with the courtship between Pentecostals, and evangelicals and mainline churches. In an attempt to gain respectability with evangelicals, Pentecostals had begun the "muting of such Pentecostal distinctives as speaking in tongues, prophesying, and praying for the sick. Along with this came a sense of dryness and aridity in many Pentecostal congregations. Although few would recognize it, by the end of World War II the American Pentecostal movement needed a renewal."[2] In the words of Rev. David Kiteley, Violet's son, the movement that "was born in fire was living on smoke."

During her visit to the Sharon Bible School, the Lord impressed upon Violet the words of the Apostle Paul to Timothy, "Do not neglect your gift, which was given you through a prophetic message when the body of elders laid their hands on you" (1 Timothy 4:14). As a result, Violet and her son embraced this new move of God. At three years old, David prayed for a wheelchair-bound man, and instantly the man was healed. Mother and son had begun their prophetic ministry together. According to Violet, "this new movement had a conviction from God that the offices of apostle, prophet, evangelist, pastor and teacher were being restored to the church [and] ... their role was to push up from the bottom (see Ephesians 4:11–13). This was, and still is, a revolutionary concept to denominations that advocated leadership from a centralized location and functioned with a top-down form of government."[3]

Although local pastors wanted Violet to continue to make sharing her testimony of healing her central ministry, she instead embraced the movement that became the "New Order of the Latter Rain." Soon she and the movement would experience opposition from established Pentecostal denominations, particularly the Assemblies of God. The result of this resistance was that "by 1950 . . . [the movement was] confined to independent churches and popular healing evangelists such as Thomas Wyatt and William Branham."[4] Long-term, the influence of the Latter Rain movement, however, would be significant in the neo-Pentecostal and Charismatic movements that emerged after 1960.

2. Synan, *Holiness-Pentecostal Tradition*, 212.
3. Kiteley, "Remembering Latter Rain," 2.
4. Synan, *Holiness-Pentecostal Tradition*, 213.

Violet continued to minister in Canada, and in 1958 she founded the Revival Tabernacle Foursquare Church. Out of her concern that individuals would have a depth of understanding of the Bible to accompany their Pentecostal experience and gifting, she established a training center that served not only her church but also those in the local community.

In September of 1965, Violet began her ministry in Oakland, California. The impetus for this move was her desire to minister to people of various ethnicities and to establish branches of the church and school she had established in Canada. The choice of Oakland couldn't have been better as it was, and continues to be, one of the most ethnically diverse cities in the United States. At first Violet held ten Bible studies a week in cities across the Bay Area, and then began Shiloh Church in the Oakland home of an African-American couple, Burrell and Eleanor Porter.

The church initially moved to a storefront in deep east Oakland at 8620 MacArthur Boulevard, and then to another on Foothill. In 1967 the congregation moved into a two-story building on 38th Avenue. With every relocation, the church kept moving closer to the geographic center of the city. Initially, Violet held services five days a week and began with a regular attendance of about twenty people. Within two years, the congregation would grow into the hundreds.

The initial wave of new converts included members of the hippie movement, Roman Catholics and those with Episcopalian and Presbyterian backgrounds. Although a Pentecostal church, the Protestant members of its original congregation were primarily from mainline churches. Most of the hippies traveled from Berkeley and the Haight-Asbury neighborhood of San Francisco to hear the message of salvation and be baptized. The church soon became a northern California center for the Jesus and Charismatic renewal movements.

As part of its outreach ministries the Shiloh Church opened the HMS Noah Coffee Shop in a storefront near the church. Decorated with a nautical theme, coffee and banana bread was served as budding Christian music groups played and the Spirit of God moved within the hearts of the patrons. In the political arena, Violet and members of the congregation marched in the civil rights movement. From her perspective, the movement for racial equality was a movement of God and not a political movement—she was "marching for righteousness." She saw the ethnic diversity in her congregation as a model for society.

Once the church was established and growing in its new location, Violet's focus shifted to education. This was especially important because, from her perspective, Pentecostals were "preached to death, but didn't know anything." Shiloh Bible College was opened in September 1967[5] with ten students and three teachers, and initially classes were offered on Saturdays. In contrast to nearby Patten Bible College (founded as Oakland Bible Institute by Bebe Patten, now Patten University), Violet did not start her school with the intention of it becoming a degree-granting institution of higher education. Instead, its focus was to impart to students knowledge of the Word of God and teach them how to live overcoming lives for Christ. God's plans, however, were greater than the original vision for the school. Shiloh Bible College currently offers both undergraduate and graduate degrees, and has satellite campuses in China (5), Ethiopia (8), Mexico (1), and Nigeria (1).

Violet's father, Albert, who took her hand and helped her as a teenager to take those first steps in ministry, continued his own healing ministry until his home-going at age 105 in 1988. Two days before his death, he was praying for the healing of an individual in his daughter's church. As she teaches in the college and participates in the ministries of the church, now pastored by her grandson, Violet's life and ministry continues to confirm that "the mantle of God is upon her."

---

5. Kiteley, *Forty Years of Increase*, 13.

27

She Guarded the Secret in Her Heart

Freda Lindsay

Freda Schimpf didn't have anything better to do one evening, so she accepted her sister's invitation to attend a revival service being held at the Portland church of Dr. John G. Lake. She had finished high school, but her family couldn't afford to send her to college. As a result, she worked as a domestic for $30 a month, and life was boringly consistent. At least that's the way it was until she attended the revival service.

The conviction of the Lord was upon her, but because she was too embarrassed to let others know that she was not a Christian, she waited until the service closed to go to the altar. It was there she found forgiveness for her sins and dedicated her life to the Lord.[1] That fateful night in 1932, Gordon Lindsay was the preacher and Freda was the only person converted that final night of the revival. God had plans for these two, because "the Lord spoke to her in a still, small voice and told her that if she would be faithful to Him, she would one day marry Gordon. Freda didn't share that promise with anyone for several years."[2]

A marriage many years before resulted in the birth of Freda Schimpf on April 18, 1914. Gottfried and Kaity, both Germans who were raised in Russia, emigrated separately to the United States where they met and were married. They soon emigrated again, this time to Canada, to take advantage of the government's offer of free land where homesteaders were expected to raise wheat. Settling near Burstall, Saskatchewan, there was

1. Bozarth, *Freda Lindsay*, 16.
2. Ibid., 18.

an immediate need to provide shelter for he and his wife, so Gottfried constructed a sod house (made from prairie grass). It was in this home that Freda, the second of their twelve children, was born.

Extreme winters led to the Schmipf's move back to America in 1919, this time to Oregon City, Oregon. Economic survival was a family enterprise, so at nine years old, Freda worked twelve-hour days during the summers picking berries and string beans. During her teenage years, she would travel to Washington State to hoe sugar beats during summers.

Gottfried had come to know the Lord while he was still in Russia, having been converted in the Lutheran church. However, once in Oregon the family attended a Full Gospel church, at which a number of them not only surrendered their lives to Jesus but were filled with the Holy Spirit. At age eighteen, Freda had joined the rest of the family in making her faith commitment.

Seven years before Freda's dramatic conversion, Gordon had attended a revival in that same Portland church. The speaker was Charles Parham, whose anointed preaching brought conviction to the young man's heart. Gordon went forward to pray at the altar and not only surrender his life to Christ but received the call to ministry. During that same year, Gordon attended the revivals of evangelist Billy Sunday and faith healer Dr. Charles S. Price, and his experiences in those services reinforced his commitment to evangelism.

Gordon and two associates began to hold evangelistic services in El Cajon, California. At the close of the revival, Gordon became ill with a near fatal case of ptomaine poisoning. Having heard of his condition, faith healer John G. Lake took Gordon into his home in San Diego. While resting, Gordon would read Dr. Lake's printed sermons on healing. Realizing his need for active faith, Gordon trusted the Lord as he prayed for his healing, and got out of bed. As his feet touched the floor, he experienced divine healing.

Having given her heart to Jesus, Freda involved herself in ministry of the Portland Foursquare Gospel Church. She was selected as president of the church's Crusader youth program. In addition to directing the youth services, she helped lead the youth in prison and street witnessing. As Freda foresaw her future as that of a minister's wife, she enrolled in the Foursquare Bible school's night classes, and during the day she worked as a department store cashier.

Four years after her conversion, Gordon showed up at the store where Freda was working and asked her out to dinner. Before he left a few days later he asked if she would answer his letters, and she said yes. One year later on November 14, 1937, they were married in front of 1,600 people by Dr. Harold Jefferies, a Portland Foursquare Church pastor and the denomination's Northwest District superintendent. A partnership in the Lord's service was born.

Freda and Gordon then traveled south to San Fernando, California, to start a church. However, because Freda only had six months' work to complete before graduating from LIFE Bible College, Gordon returned to the evangelistic field while Freda completed her studies. Although there was resistance to this decision from family members, the newlyweds felt that this was the Lord's timing. When Freda graduated, she assisted Gordon with his evangelistic campaigns.

The itinerary and ministry role of this evangelistic couple expanded, as they first served as pastors of a church on an interim basis in Tacoma, Washington, and then began to plant a church in Billings, Montana. Their "home" consisted of two second-story rooms above an uncompleted tabernacle, and because of the slant of the roof they could only stand upright in the center of one of the rooms. Freda and Gordon put their full effort to accomplish two goals: grow a church and finish the construction of the sanctuary building. During services, Gordon preached and played the piano, and Freda served as song leader, youth and Sunday school director, and janitor.

Unfortunately, Freda became ill, first experiencing symptoms of a cold, but then her weight dropped to about ninety-four pounds. Gordon then drove Freda to her mother's home in Portland to recuperate, and after a couple of days traveled back to California to continue the work at the church. Freda's condition worsened and she was diagnosed with tuberculosis in both lungs. Gordon returned to his wife's side, reading to her 1 John 3:21 ("Beloved, if our heart does not condemn, we have confidence toward God") and assured her that it was God's will to heal her. After they both spent time in prayer, Gordon prayed a prayer of faith for Freda's healing. She felt God's healing touch and got out of bed, and two weeks later the couple was back in Billings.

Freda and Gordon returned to evangelistic endeavors, and soon began their family. Carole Ann was born in 1940, the same year that Gordon published *The Wonders of Bible Chronology*, the first of 250 books he would write in his lifetime. In the midst of World War II, in 1943, their second child Gilbert was born. The couple settled down for a while in Ashland, Oregon, to pastor a small Assemblies of God church there. Four years later their third child, Dennis, was born.

In 1947, Gordon and Jack Moore began publishing *The Voice of Healing*, initially intended to keep readers informed of revivals that were part of the ministry of Baptist pastor William Branham. When Branham stepped away from the evangelistic field because of health reasons, he handed *The Voice of Healing* over to Gordon. He turned the magazine's use to report on evangelistic and healing ministries prevalent at the time, including those of Oral Roberts, Kenneth Hagin, Rudy Cerrulo and others.

During this time Freda added teaching to her duties, as she homeschooled their children. This task was added to attending two meetings a day, leading worship and helping Gordon prepare content for *The Voice of Healing* as they traveled. In 1952 Dallas was selected as the headquarters for their ministry, and Gordon entrusted Freda with all the business aspects of the ministry. This enabled Gordon the freedom to "speak in conventions, and seminars, write books, serve as editor of the magazine, and oversee the worldwide foreign mission endeavors."[3] Their ministry grew, and in 1967 *The Voice of Healing* (the name of their ministry as well as the magazine) was changed to *Christ for the Nations*, to reflect the global reach of the ministry.

In 1970, Gordon shared with Freda that he felt they should start a Bible school. Freda was at first reluctant because Gordon was in his mid-sixties and she was concerned about the impact taking on such a new endeavor would have on his health. Undeterred, he convinced Freda, and Christ for the Nations Institute opened its doors in September of 1970 with a beginning class of fifty students.

Three years later, Freda's life would take a dramatic turn. On April 1, 1973, Christ for the Nations was celebrating Gordon's twenty-fifth year as president of the ministry. In the midst of giving announcements, Freda turned toward her beloved husband and he appeared to be sleeping. In truth, he had gone home to be with the Lord.

Although stunned by her husband's sudden death, Freda remained determined that the ministries she and Gordon had started would con-

---

3. Walker, "Destined to Touch the Nations," 22.

tinue. The day after the funeral, the ten-man board voted unanimously to make Freda Gordon's successor. She immediately wrote to all the missionaries and national workers affiliated with the ministry assuring them that all projects Christ for the Nations had begun would be completed.

As the fall semester was approaching for the school, Freda was very concerned about enrollment for its second year. But instead of dropping, enrollment doubled. The $750,000 needed to buy the property and constructing the building and parking was raised in two years. Freda also became the editor of *Christ for the Nations* magazine. The Christ for the Nations Native Church program continued, and eventually assisted more than 10,000 congregations in developing countries to complete their church facilities. Bible schools in Argentina, Finland, Germany, India, Indonesia, Kenya, Peru, South Africa, Sri Lanka, Thailand, and Zimbabwe have been established by Christ for the Nations.

Freda's leadership and faithfulness to ministry were recognized in various ways. In 1977 she was awarded an honorary doctorate of divinity at the International Foursquare Convention in Portland, Oregon. Six years later she was named "Christian Woman of the Year." In 1987, she was awarded a Doctor of Humane Letters degree from Oral Roberts University.

Freda's life is a testimony to her oft-stated philosophy: "Life is not a sprint. Life is a marathon—a cross-country, disciplined commitment to win the eternal Olympics." Her ministerial efforts were at first a solo effort, later a dual one completed in harmony with her husband, and unfortunately returned to a solo with Gordon's home-going. However, the legacy of Freda and Gordon continues.

From humble beginnings, Freda and Gordon became "leaders of the healing movement, publishers, editors, founders and directors of the Christ for the Nations Institute ... and made major contributions to interdenominational and interconfessional understanding among Pentecostals and charismatics."[4]

---

4. Bundy, "Freda Theresa and Gordon Lindsay," 842.

Conclusion

Women's history in this country is one in which men believed that women had no place in the academy. Within this context, for a woman to step into a classroom as a student, teacher, or administrator she would clearly be stepping out of her place. The "great cloud of witnesses" (Hebrews 12:1) presented in this book is a testimony to women who, in the face of cultural, religious, and societal barriers, made their mark on the landscape of American higher education.

Women in the Wesleyan Holiness and Pentecostal movements joined their sisters from other faith traditions and walks of life to prove over and again that women have a significant role to play in the founding, developing, and sustaining institutions of higher education. Their efforts are part of a continuum in which women both advocated for and seized their place in the "public sphere" of education.

For women from the Wesleyan Holiness and Pentecostal traditions, the experience of sanctification and the empowerment resulting from the baptism of the Holy Spirit served as catalysts for them to embrace their identity in the area of public ministry. Thus empowered, these women were able to face and conquer challenges, both personal and professional, in establishing Bible institutes, deaconess and missionary training schools, and Bible colleges and seminaries.

They demonstrated mental acumen in curriculum planning, selecting personnel, facility development, business decision-making, fundraising, and administrative leadership. It is significant to note that for many of these women, founding an educational institution was just one of the accomplishments in their lives. Their ministry also led to the founding of orphanages, rescue missions, faith homes, social work ministries, missionary efforts, churches and denominations.

These women demonstrated that they not only had the mental capacity to think about "things theological," but were able to establish schools where theological thought and application is the central activity.

Appendix

Timeline of Wesleyan Holiness and Pentecostal Founders

Year	Name	Faith Tradition	School Founded	School Today
1855	Eliza Garrett	WH	Garrett Biblical Institute	Garrett Evangelical Theological Seminary
1883	Emma Dryer	WH	May Institute	Moody Bible Institute
1885	Lucy Rider Meyer	WH	Chicago Training School	Merged with the Garrett Biblical Institute in 1934
1887	Emma Dryer	WH	Chicago Evangelism Society	Moody Bible Institute
1894	Carrie Judd Montgomery	WH/P	Shalom Training School	
1900	Philena Hadley, Mary Hill, Elizabeth Harper, M. Anna Draper, Bertha Pinkham, Matilda W. Atkinson	WH	Training School for Christian Workers	Azusa Pacific University
1900	Fannie Suddarth	WH	Arkansas Holiness College	Southern Nazarene University
1901	Iva Vennard	WH	Epworth Evangelistic Institute	closed
1902	Bible College Prayer Circle (included Leona Maris, R. C. Ruth, Martha L. Seymour)	WH	Pacific Bible College	Point Loma Nazarene
1905 (Circa)	Mary Lee Cagle	WH	Bible School	

Appendix

Year	Name	Faith Tradition	School Founded	School Today
1905	Mattie Hoke	WH	Apostolic Holiness Bible School	Bresee College of the Southern Nazarene University
1906	Mattie Mallory	WH	Beulah Heights College and Bible School	Southern Nazarene University
1906	Elizabeth Baker	P	Rochester Bible Training School	
1908	Alma White	WH	Zarephath Bible Institute	Somerset Christian College
1910	Iva Vennard	WH	Chicago Evangelistic Institute	Vennard College, closed in 2008
1912	Virginia Moss	P	Beulah Heights Bible and Missionary Training School	
1916	Minnie Draper	P	Bethel Bible Training School	Merged with Central Bible Institute in 1929
1917	Alma White	WH	Alma White College	closed in 1978
1918	Nora Chambers	P	Bible Training School	Lee University
1919	Mary Craig	P	Pacific Bible Institute	Bethany University
1920	Alma White	WH	Belleview Christian College and Seminary	Belleview College
1923	Aimee Semple McPherson	P	Echo Park Evangelistic and Missionary Training Institute	Life Pacific College
1924	Christine A. Gibson	P	Mount Zion Bible School	Zion Bible College
1926	Alice Luce	P	Berean Bible Institute	Latin American Bible Institute
1930	Lela McConnell	WH	Kentucky Mountain Bible Institute	Kentucky Mountain Bible College
1937	Ruth Kerr[1]	WH	Bible Missionary Institute	Westmont College
1940	Mary Keith	P	Keith Bible Institute	
1944	Bebe Patten	P	Oakland Bible Institute	Patten University
1957	Alta Washburn	P	All Tribes Bible School	American Indian College

1. Ruth Kerr was a Baptist most of her life.

Timeline of Wesleyan Holiness and Pentecostal Founders

Year	Name	Faith Tradition	School Founded	School Today
1967	Violet Kiteley	P	Shiloh Bible College	Shiloh Bible College
1970	Freda Lindsay	P	Christ for the Nations Institute	Christ for the Nations Institute

WH: Wesleyan Holiness

P: Pentecostal

Bibliography

Alexander, Estrelda. *Limited Liberty: The Legacy of Four Pentecostal Women Pioneers.* Cleveland, TN: Pilgrim, 2008.
Alexander, Estrelda, and Amos Yong, editors. *Philip's Daughters: Women in Pentecostal-Charismatic Leadership.* Eugene, OR: Pickwick, 2009.
Alexander, Kimberly Ervin, and R. Hollis Gause. *Women in Leadership: A Pentecostal Perspective.* Cleveland, TN: Center for Pentecostal Leadership & Care, 2006.
Alvarez, Carmelo. "Hispanic Pentecostals: Azusa Street and Beyond." *Cyberjournal for Pentecostal-Charismatic Research*, February 1999. Online: http://www.pctii.org/cyberj/cyberj5/alvarez.html.
"At Rest from Her Labor." *The Christian Evangel* 298/299 (July 26, 1919) 9.
Azusa Pacific University. "Our History." Online: http://www.apu.edu/about/history.
Baker, Elizabeth V. *Chronicles of Faith.* New York: Garland, 1984.
Baker, Elizabeth V., et al. *Chronicles of a Faith Life.* 2nd ed. Rochester, NY: Elim, 1926.
Bass, Clarence B. *Backgrounds to Dispensationalism: Its Historical Genesis and Ecclesiastical Implications.* Grand Rapids: Baker, 1960.
Beecher, Catherine E. *The Duty of American Women to Their Country.* New York: Harper, 1845.
"Bethany College: 85 Years Aflame." News release, September 21, 2004. Online: http://ag.org/top/News/index_articledetail.cfm?Process=DisplayArticle&targetBay=ea7fb5b4-34e2-4cd7-99a1-b7ce6556476b&ModID=2&RSS_RSSContentID=3391&RSS_OriginatingChannelID=1184&RSS_OriginatingRSSFeedID=3359&RSS_Source=search.
Beulah Heights College and Bible School: Second Annual Catalogue (1907–8). Oklahoma City, 1907.
"Bishop Mary F. L. Keith." Online: http://www.houseofgod.ws/html_files/BishopKeith.html.
Blackstone, William, Sir. *Commentaries on the Laws of England.* Vol. 1. Oxford: Clarendon, 1765.
Blumhofer, Edith L. "Agnes Nevada Ozman." In *The New International Dictionary of Pentecostal and Charismatic Movements*, edited by Stanley M. Burgess and Eduard M. Der Maas, 952. Grand Rapids: Zondervan, 2002.
———. *Aimee Semple McPherson: Everybody's Sister.* Grand Rapids: Eerdmans, 1993.
———. *The Assemblies of God: A Chapter in the Story of American Pentecostalism.* Vol. 1: *To 1941.* Springfield, MI: Gospel Publishing House, 1989.
———. "Life on the Faith Lines: Faith Homes and Early Pentecostal Values." *Assemblies of God Heritage* 10:2 (Summer 1990) 10–12, 22.
———. *Restoring the Faith: The Assemblies of God, Pentecostalism and American Culture.* Champaign: University of Illinois Press, 1993.

Bibliography

Bowie, Mary Ella. *Alabaster and Spikenard: The Life of Iva Durham Vennard, D.D., Founder of Chicago Evangelistic Institute*. Chicago: Chicago Evangelistic Institute, 1947.

Bozarth, Randy, compiler. *Freda Lindsay: Life and Teachings*. Dallas: World Missions Advance, 2007.

Brown, I. C. *"In Their Times": A History of the Chicago Training School on the Occasion of Its Centennial Celebration, 1885–1985*. Evanston, IL: Garrett Evangelical Theological Seminary, n.d.

Bundy, D. D. "Freda Theresa and Gordon Lindsay." In *The New International Dictionary of Pentecostal and Charismatic Movements*, edited by Stanley M. Burgess and Eduard M. Der Maas, 841–42. Grand Rapids: Zondervan, 2002.

Buoy, Charles Wesley. *Representative Women of Methodism, 1841–1897*. New York: Hunt & Eaton; Cincinnati: Cranston & Curts, 1893.

Cagle, Mary Lee. *Life and Work of Mary Lee Cagle*. Kansas City: Nazarene Publishing House, 1928.

Callen, Barry L. *Discerning the Divine God in Christian Theology*. Louisville, KY: Westminster John Knox, 2004

Carroll, Geneva. "Youth Interviews Experience." *The Lighted Pathway Yearbook* 14 (1949) n.p.

Casey, Lee. "Bishop White." *Rocky Mountain News*, June 28, 1946, 14.

Chambers, F. G. "A Brief Sketch of Our Work in the Mountains of North Carolina and Georgia." Unpublished.

The Children's Center. "Our Mission and History." Online: http://www.tccokc.org/index.php?option=com_content&task=view&id=114&Itemid=215.

"Church of God General Assembly Minutes." Union Grove, TN, January 10, 1907.

"Church of God Evangelist License." Issued to Nora Chambers on August 20, 1910.

"Church of the Nazarene." *The Encyclopedia of Arkansas History and Culture*. Online: http://www.encyclopediaofarkansas.net/encyclopedia/entry-detail.aspx?entryID=4330.

Clark, D. W. "Mrs. Eliza Garrett." In *Our Excellent Women of the Methodist Church in England and America*, edited by Gabriel P. Disoway, 201–9. New York: J. C. Buttre, 1861.

"To Close Revival." Unknown publication, July 26, 1947.

Conn, Charles W. *Like a Mighty Army Moves the Church of God*. Cleveland, TN: Church of God Pub. House, 1955.

———. *Where the Saints Have Trod: A History of Church of God Missions*. Cleveland, TN: Pathway, 1959.

"CORPORATIONS: The Lord Helps Those . . ." *Time Magazine*, February 21, 1949. Online: http://www.time.com/time/magazine/article/0,9171,805089,00.html.

Cott, Nancy F., editor. *No Small Courage: A History of Women in the United States*. Oxford: Oxford University Press, 2000.

Craig, Mary. "A Word from the Founder." *Tidings* (yearbook of the Glad Tidings Bible Institute), 1938, 5.

Crews, Mickey. *The Church of God: A Social History*. Knoxville: University of Tennessee Press, 1990.

Curtis, Heather D. *Faith in the Great Physician: Suffering and Divine Healing in American Culture, 1860–1900*. Baltimore: John Hopkins University Press, 2007.

"DeJernett, Rev. E. C." *Wesley United Methodist Church History 1850–2000, Pastors*. N.d., n.p. Online: http://freepages.history.rootsweb.ancestry.com/~huntnews/wesley%20church/DeJernettEC.pdf.

Bibliography

De Leon, Victor. *The Silent Pentecostals: A Biographical History of the Pentecostal Movement in the Twentieth Century*. Taylors, SC: Faith Printing, 1979.

Dieter, Melvin E. *The Holiness Revival of the Nineteenth Century*. 2nd ed. Lanham, MD: Scarecrow, 1996.

Dirksen, Carolyn Rowland. "Let Your Women Keep Silence." In *The Promise and the Power: Essays on the Motivations, Developments and Prospects of the Ministries of the Church of God*, edited by Donald N. Bowdle, 165–96. Cleveland, TN: Pathway, 1980.

Disoway, Gabriel P. *Our Excellent Women of the Methodist Church in England and America*. New York: J. C. Buttre, 1861.

Draper, Minnie Tingley. "God's Desire." *The Christian Alliance and Foreign Missionary Weekly*, May 18, 1894, 547.

"Emeline Dryer: Christian Educator and Administrator." *History's Women—The Unsung Heroines*. Online: http://www.historywomen.com/womenoffaith/EmelineDryer.html.

The Encyclopedia of Arkansas History and Culture. Online: http://www.encyclopediaofarkansas.net.

Espinosa, Gaston. "Third Class Soldiers." In *Philip's Daughters: Women in Pentecostal-Charismatic Leadership*, edited by Estrelda Alexander and Amos Young, 95–111. Eugene, OR: Pickwick, 2009.

———. "'Your Daughters Shall Prophesy': A History of Women in Ministry in the Latino Pentecostal Movement in the United States." In *Women and Twentieth-Century Protestantism*, edited by Margaret Lamberts Brendroth and Virginia Lieson Brereton, 25–48. Urbana: University of Illinois Press, 2002.

Fisher, Alice. "Overflowing with Thankfulness." Unpublished, 1994.

Fisher, Ila Alexander. "Eliza Garrett: To Follow a Vision." In *Spirituality and Social Responsibility: Vocational Vision of Women in the United Methodist Tradition*, edited by Rosemary Skinner Keller, 41–59. Nashville: Abingdon, 1993.

Foreman, Carolyn Thomas. *Oklahoma Imprints, 1835-1907: A History of Printing in Oklahoma before Statehood*. Norman: University of Oklahoma Press, 1936.

Garrett, Augustus. Letter to Jerry Clark, January 15, 1845. In "Letterbook," 1. 1843–45. Northwestern University archives.

Glad Tidings Church. "Our History." Online: http://gtsf.org/our-history/.

Golder, C. *History of the Deaconess Movement in the Christian Church*. Cincinnati: Jennings and Pye, 1908.

Gorbacheva, Tatiana. "Nora Chambers—Education Pioneer." *Church of God History and Heritage*, Fall 1997, 3–5.

Gresham, Loren P., and L. Paul Gresham. *From Many Came One, In Jesus' Name: Southern Nazarene University Looks Back on a Century*. Virginia Beach, VA: Donning, 1998.

Harmon, Sandra D. "Women Building Chicago: Illinois State Normal University Connections." *Women's Voice* 7:4 (November/December 2001) 1–2.

Harris, Merne A. "An Elect Lady: Some Reflections upon the Life and Ministry of Iva Durham Vennard." *Holiness Digest*, Fall 1999. Online: http://www.whwomenclergy.org/articles/article9.php.

Harvey, T. W. Letter to Nettie McCormick, July 19, 1888. In *Sin in the City: Chicago and Revivalism, 1880-1920*, by Thelka Ellen Joiner, 59. Columbia: University of Missouri Press, 2007.

Harvey, E. F., and E. Hey. *They Knew Their God*. Vol. 1. Hampton, TN: Harvey Christian, 2003.

Bibliography

Higgenbotham, Evelyn Brooks. *Righteous Discontent: The Women's Movement in the Black Baptist Church, 1880–1920*. Cambridge: Harvard University Press, 1993.

Hill, Jerry D., and T. G. Shuck. *Kentucky Weather*. Lexington: University Press of Kentucky, 2005.

Hill, Mary. "Interdenominational Character." In *1900–1901 Catalogue and Prospectus of the Training School for Christian Workers*, n.p. 1900.

———. "Mary Hill 1901 Write Up." 1901.

Hoke, Mattie. "Hitherto Hath the Lord Helped Us." In *Second Annual Catalogue of the Apostolic Holiness Bible School: 1907–08*, 7–8. Hutchinson, KS, 1907.

Horton, Isabelle. *The Burden of the City*. New York: Revell, 1904.

———. *High Adventure: Life of Lucy Rider Meyer*. New York: Methodist Book Concern, 1928.

The House of God Church. "Celebrating 100 Years of Holiness, 1903–2003." Centennial Celebration. Nashville, 2003.

Hunter, Fannie McDowell. *Women Preachers*. Women and Church in America 85. Dallas: Berachah, 1905.

Ingersol, Stan. "Mattie Mallory for the Children." *Herald of Holiness*, August 1995, 35. Online: http://www.whwomenclergy.org/articles/article18.php.

———. "Why These Schools? Historical Perspectives on Nazarene Higher Education." Online: http://www.nazarene.org/files/docs/Why%20These%20Schools%20%20Historical%20Perspectives%20on%20Nazarene%20Higher%20Education.pdf.

Irwin, Benjamin H. "The Central Idea." *Live Coals of Fire*, November 10, 1899, 4.

Jackson, Sheldon, and Tamsen Murray. "Azusa Pacific University." In *Founded by Friends: The Quaker Heritage of Fifteen American Colleges and Universities*, edited by John W. Oliver Jr., Charles L. Cherry, and Caroline L. Cherry, 241–51. Lanham, MD: Scarecrow, 2007.

Joiner, Thekla Ellen. *Sin in the City: Chicago and Revivalism 1880–1920*. Columbia: University of Missouri Press, 2007.

Jones, Charles Edwin. "The Oklahoma Orphanage and the Founding of Bethany." *The Chronicles of Oklahoma* 71:4 (Winter 1993–94) 392–421.

———. "Zion Evangelistic Fellowship." In *The New International Dictionary of Pentecostal and Charismatic Movements*, edited by Stanley M. Burgess and Eduard M. Der Maas, 1226. Grand Rapids: Zondervan, 2002.

Kirkermo, Ronald B. *For Zion's Sake: A History of Pasadena/Point Loma College*. San Diego: Point Loma Press, 1992.

Kiteley, David. *Forty Years of Increase: The Shiloh Miracle*. Kearney, NE: Morris, 2005.

Kiteley, Violet. "Remembering the Latter Rain." *SpiritLed Woman*, August/September 2000. Online: http://www.spiritledwoman.com/display.php?id=500.

Kunkel, Glenn. *Winning the Race: Bebe Patten, Her Life and Ministry*. Cleveland, TN: Pathway, 2000.

Laird, Rebecca. *Ordained Women in the Church of the Nazarene: The First Generation*. Kansas City: Nazarene Publishing House, 1993.

Lawson, Steven. "Kiteley Family a Point of Light in Troubled Oakland." *Charisma*, January 2003. Online: http://www.charismamag.com/index.php/component/content/article/268-people-and-events/7035-kiteley-family-a-point-of-light-in-troubled-oakland.

Lee, S. D. "Evangelical Domesticity: The Women's Temperance Crusade of 1873–1874." In *Women in New Worlds*, edited by Rosemary Skinner Keller, Louise L. Queen, and Hilah F. Thomas, 1:293–309. Nashville: Abingdon, 1981.

Bibliography

Lewis, Meharry H. *Mary Lena Lewis Tate: "A Street Called Straight."* Chattanooga, TN: New and Living Way, 2002.

———. *Mary Lena Lewis Tate: Vision!* Chattanooga, TN: New and Living Way, 2005.

Lincoln, C. Eric, and Lawrence H. Mamiya. *The Black Church in the African American Experience.* Durham: Duke University Press, 1990.

Lindley, Susan Hill. *"You Have Stept out of Your Place": A History of Women and Religion in America.* Louisville: Westminster John Knox, 1996.

Lindsay, Freda. *A Book of Miracles: Providential, Promised, Provision, Provided.* Dallas: Christ for the Nations, 1996.

———. *Freda: The Widow Who Took Up the Mantle.* Dallas: Christ for the Nations Inc., 1984.

"Location." In *Kansas Holiness Institute and Bible School: 1911–1912 Catalog*, 5. Hutchinson, KS, 1911.

Lucas, C. J. "In Memoriam." *Full Gospel Missionary Herald*, April 1921, 4.

Luce, Alice. "The Latin American Pentecostal Work." *Pentecostal Evangel*, June 25, 1927, 7.

———. "Scriptural Methods in Missionary Work." *Pentecostal Evangel*, May 9, 1931, 8–9.

McConnell, Lela. *The Pauline Ministry in the Kentucky Mountains.* Berne, IN: Economy Printing Concern, 1942.

———. *Rewarding Faith plus Works.* Vancleeve, KY: Kentucky Mountain Bible Institute, 1962.

McGee, Gary B. "Alice Eveline Luce." In *The New International Dictionary of Pentecostal and Charismatic Movements*, edited by Stanley M. Burgess and Eduard M. Der Maas, 844–45. Grand Rapids: Zondervan, 2002.

———. "Elizabeth V. Baker." In *The New International Dictionary of Pentecostal and Charismatic Movements*, edited by Stanley M. Burgess and Eduard M. Der Maas, 351–52. Grand Rapids: Zondervan, 2002.

———. "This Gospel Shall Be Preached: The Beginning Years for Pioneer Assemblies of God Missionaries." *Assemblies of God Heritage* (Winter 1986–87) 6–8, 10.

———. "Three Notable Women in Pentecostal Ministry." *Assemblies of God Heritage* (Spring 1985–86) 3–5, 12, 16.

———. "Virginia E. Moss." In *The New International Dictionary of Pentecostal and Charismatic Movements*, edited by Stanley M. Burgess and Eduard M. Der Maas, 909. Grand Rapids: Zondervan, 2002.

McGill, Alexander T. "The Present Age, the Age of Woman: An Address before the Literary Societies of Oxford Female College, at Their Anniversary." Oxford, June 24, 1858.

McMillen, Sally G. *Seneca Falls and the Origins of the Women's Rights Movement.* Oxford: Oxford University Press, 2008.

McPherson, Aimee. *The Story of My Life.* Hollywood, CA: International Correspondents, 1951.

Meyer, Rider Lucy. *Deaconesses, Biblical, Early Church, European, American.* Cincinnati: Cranston & Stowe, 1892.

Moncher, Gary Richard. "The Bible College and American Moral Culture." PhD diss., University of California at Berkeley, 1987.

Moss, Virginia E. *Following the Shepherd.* North Bergen, NJ: Beulah Heights Bible Training School, 1923. Item 64185, Flower Pentecostal Heritage Center, Springfield, MO.

Mulliken, Charles H. "Sixty-Second Report of the Chicago Bible Society for the Year 1901." Chicago, 1902.

"Mystery Fire Hits Bebe Patten Home." *Oakland Post Inquirer*, March 9, 1949, 1.

Bibliography

"No More Church Fund Work: 'Cash' Patten to be Paroled in August." *San Francisco Chronicle*, February 18, 1953, n.p.

Norwood, Frederick A. *Dawn to Midday at Garrett*. Evanston, IL: Garrett-Evangelical Theological Seminary, 1978.

"Obituary—Hoke." *Herald of Holiness* (April 16, 1838) 158.

"Old Orchard Convention." *The Christian Missionary Alliance* (August 25, 1906) 125.

Opp, James W. "Healing Hands, Healthy Bodies: Protestant Women and Faith Healing in Canada and the United States, 1880–1930." In *Women and Twentieth-Century Protestantism*, edited by Margaret Lamberts Brendroth and Virginia Lieson Brereton, 236–56. Urbana: University of Illinois Press, 2002.

Otto, Ken. *Azusa Pacific University*. Charleston, SC: Arcadia, 2008.

Pacific Bible College. *Third Annual Catalog, 1904–05*.

Palmer, Phoebe. *The Way of Holiness, with Notes by the Way; Being a Narrative of Religious Experience Resulting from a Determination to Be a Bible Christian*. New York: G. Lane & C. B. Tippett, 1845.

"Patten Trial Is Ordered to Move to Hospital Tomorrow." *Oakland Tribune* (June 26, 1950) 1.

Patterson, Eric, and Edmund Rybarczyk, editors. *The Future of Pentecostalism in the United States*. Lanham, MD: Lexington Books, 2007.

Pope-Levison, Priscilla. "Iva Durham Vennard: 1871–1945." *Prism*, September/October 2005, 3.

———. *Turn the Pulpit Loose: Two Centuries of American Women Evangelists*. New York: Palgave McMillan, 2004.

Prelinger, Catherine M., and Rosemary S. Keller. "The Function of Female Bonding: The Restored Diaconessate of the Nineteenth Century." In *Women in New Worlds*, edited by Rosemary Skinner Keller, Louise L. Queen, and Hilah F. Thomas, 2:318–37. Nashville: Abingdon, 1982.

"Program: Memorial Services Held for Mrs. Ruth K. Kerr." Westmont College, Santa Barbara, CA, November/December 1967.

Riss, Richard M. *A Survey of 20th Century Revival Movements in North America*. Peabody, MA: Hendrickson, 1988.

Robeck, Cecil M., Jr. "Aimee Semple McPherson." In *The New International Dictionary of Pentecostal and Charismatic Movements*, edited by Stanley M. Burgess and Eduard M. Der Maas, 856–58. Grand Rapids: Zondervan, 2002.

———. "International Church of the Foursquare Gospel." In *The New International Dictionary of Pentecostal and Charismatic Movements*, edited by Stanley M. Burgess and Eduard M. Der Maas, 793–94. Grand Rapids: Zondervan, 2002.

———. *The Azusa Street Mission and Revival: The Birth of the Global Pentecostal Movement*. Nashville: T. Nelson, 2006.

Robert, Dana L. *American Women in Mission: A Social History of Their Thought and Practice*. Macon, GA: Mercer University Press, 1997.

Saggio, Joseph J. "Alta M. Washburn: An Iconoclastic Pentecostal 'Trailblazer' to the Tribes." Paper presented at the 27th Annual Meeting of the Society for Pentecostal Studies, Duke University, March 2008.

———. "Alta M. Washburn: 'Trailblazer' to the Tribes." *Assemblies of God Heritage* 27 (2007) 28–33.

Sánchez Walsh, Arlene M. *Latino Pentecostal Identity: Evangelical Faith, Self, and Society*. New York: Columbia University Press, 2003

Bibliography

Second Annual Catalogue of the Apostolic Holiness Bible School: 1907–08. 1907.

Sklar, Kathryn Kish. "The Founding of Mt. Holyoke College." In *Women of America: A History*, by Carol Ruth Berkin and Mary Beth Norton, 179–80. Boston: Houghton Mifflin, 1979.

Smith, Timothy. *Called unto Holiness: The Story of the Nazarenes—The Formative Years.* Kansas City: Nazarene Publishing House, 1962.

Stanley, Susie. "Alma White: The Politics of Dissent." In *Portraits of a Generation: Early Pentecostal Leaders*, edited by James R. Goff Jr. and Grant Wacker, 71–83. Fayetteville: University of Arkansas Press, 2002.

———. *Feminist Pillar of Fire: The Life of Alma White.* Eugene, OR: Wipf & Stock, 1993.

———. *Holy Boldness: Women Preachers' Autobiographies and the Sanctified Self.* Knoxville: University of Tennessee Press, 2002.

———. "The Promise Fulfilled: Women's Ministries in the Wesleyan/Holiness Movement." In *Religious Institutions and Women's Leadership: New Roles Inside the Mainstream*, edited by Catherine Wessinger, 139–57. Columbia: University of South Carolina Press, 1996.

Stevens, Abel. *The Women of Methodism: Memoirs of Its Three Foundresses, Susana Wesley, the Countess of Huntingdon, and Barbara Heck.* New York: Carlton and Porter, 1866.

Storms, Jeannette. "Carrie Judd Montgomery: The Little General." In *Portraits of a Generation: Early Pentecostal Leaders*, edited by James R. Goff Jr. and Grant Wacker, 271–88. Fayetteville: University of Arkansas Press, 2002.

Sutton, Matthew Avery. *Aimee Semple McPherson and the Resurrection of Christian America.* Cambridge: Harvard University Press, 2007.

Sweet, Leonard. "The Female Seminary Movement and Women's Mission in Antebellum America." *Church History* 54 (1985) 41–55.

Synan, Vinson. *The Holiness-Pentecostal Tradition: Charismatic Movements in the Twentieth Century.* Grand Rapids: Eerdmans, 1997.

Thomas, Anna. "Introduction." In "Foreign Missions Work of American Friends: A Brief History of Their Work from the Beginning to the Year Nineteen Hundred and Twelve," 1. American Board of Foreign Mission, 1912.

Thomas, Hilah F., Rosemary Skinner Keller, and Louise L. Queen, editors. *Women in New Worlds.* Nashville: Abingdon, 1981.

Thompson, A. E. *The Life of A. B. Simpson.* New York: Christian Alliance Publishing, 1920.

Tomlinson, A. J. "Better Obey God Than Listen to Man." *The Evening Light and Church of God Evangel*, May 15, 1910, 2.

"Tots Feted as Wife Now Dead, Promised." *Oregonian*, December 26, 1911.

Tucker, Ruth A., and Walter Liefeld. *Daughters of the Church: Women and Ministry from New Testament Times to the Present.* Grand Rapids: Zondervan, 1987.

Ulrich, Laurel Thatcher. "John Winthrop's City of Women." *The Massachusetts Historical Review* 3 (2001). Online: http://www.historycooperative.org/journals/mhr/3/ulrich.html.

Van De Walle, Bernie A. *The Heart of the Gospel: A. B. Simpson, the Fourfold Gospel, and Late Nineteenth Century Evangelical Theology.* Princeton Theological Monography Series 106. Eugene, OR: Pickwick, 2009.

Vandewarker, Edith. *The Mountain Shall Be Thine: The Autobiography of Lela. G. McConnell.* Vancleve, KY: Kentucky Mountain Holiness Association, 1989.

Bibliography

Vennard, Iva Durham. "Thou Are Come to the Kingdom for Such a Time as This." *Heart and Life*, October/November 1911, 6, 8. B. L. Fisher Library, Asbury Theological Seminary.

Wacker, Grant. *Heaven Below: Early Pentecostals and American Culture*. Cambridge: Harvard University Press, 2001.

Walker, Rebecca. "Destined to Touch the Nations." In *Freda Lindsay: Life and Teachings*, edited by Randy Bozareth, 15–35. Dallas: World Missions Advance, 2007.

Warner, W. E. "Carrie Judd Montgomery." In *The New International Dictionary of Pentecostal and Charismatic Movements*, edited by Stanley M. Burgess and Eduard M. Der Maas, 904–6. Grand Rapids: Zondervan, 2002.

Washburn, Alta M. *Trail to the Tribes*. Prescott, AZ, 1990.

———. Undated correspondence.

Wessinger, Catherine, editor. *Religious Institutions and Women's Leadership: New Roles Inside the Mainstream*. Columbia: University of South Carolina Press, 1996.

"When God Was Dearest to Me: A Symposium." Cleveland, TN: *The Lighted Pathway* 22:10 (October 1951) 14.

White, Alma. *The Story of My Life and the Pillar of Fire*. 6 vols. Zarephath, NJ: Pillar of Fire, 1919–34.

White, Deborah Gray. *Ar'n't I a Woman?* New York: Norton, 1999.

White, Ellen G. *The Acts of the Apostles in the Proclamation of the Gospel of Jesus Christ*. Portland, OR: Pacific Press Publishing, 1911.

Wilson, Everett A. "Robert J. Craig's Glad Tidings and the Realization of a Vision for 100,000 Souls." *Assemblies of God Heritage* 8:2 (1988) 9–11, 19.

Wilson, Everett A., and Darlene Little. *75 Years of Dreams . . . of Destiny: Glad Tidings Bible Institute, Bethany Bible College*. Scotts Valley, CA: Bethany University, 1994.

Wilson, Everett A., and Ruth Marshall Wilson. "Alice Luce: A Visionary Victorian." In *Portraits of a Generation: Early Pentecostal Leaders*, edited by James R. Goff Jr. and Grant Wacker, 159–76. Fayetteville: University of Arkansas Press, 2002.

Wilson, L. F. "Bible Institutes, Colleges, Universities." In *The New International Dictionary of Pentecostal and Charismatic Movements*, edited by Stanley M. Burgess and Eduard M. Der Maas, 372–80. Grand Rapids: Zondervan, 2002.

Wilson, Mary Campbell. *The Obedience of Faith: The Story of Rev. Christine A. Gibson, Founder of Zion Bible Institute*. Tulsa, OK: Victory House, 1993.

Wilt, Paul C. "Westmont College: A Vision, a College, a Campus." Pamphlet, May 2008.

———. "Ruth Kalbus Kerr (1894–1967)." Unpublished.

"The Word Will Keep Them." *Tidings* (1937) 6–7.

Index

Academy of Christian Education, 131
All Tribes Assemblies of God, 137–38
All Tribes Indian Bible Training School, 137
American Bible Society, 10, 97
American Indian College of the Assemblies of God, 138
Angelus Temple, 110
Apostolic Holiness Bible School, 46
Apostolic Light, 120
Arkansas Holiness College, 21, 23
Asbury College, 21, 61–63
Assemblies of God, 77, 89, 93–94, 101, 121, 134–37, 140–41, 147
Atkinson, Matilda W., 28
Azusa Pacific University, 28, 37
Azusa Street Revival, 83, 92, 117
Baker, Elizabeth V., 79–84, 115

Ball, Henry C., 118, 120
Ball (Marshall), Sunshine, 77, 118
Berean Bible Institute, 119
Beecher, Catherine, xviii
Bethany Nazarene College, 22
Bethany University, 101, 104–5, 118
Bethel Bible School, 124
Bethel Bible Training School, 93–94
Bethel Pentecostal Assembly, 92
Beulah Heights Bible and Missionary Training School, 89
Beulah Heights College and Bible School, 52–53
Beulah Heights community, 51

Bible College Prayer Circle, 34–38
The Bible-Missionary Institute, 69
Bible Training School, 99
Bible Work of Chicago, 9–12
Booth, Evangeline, 108
Booth, William and Catherine, 75, 108
Boxer Rebellion, 27, 37
Bresee College, 47
Bresee, Phineas Franklin, 34–38, 44
The Bridal Call, 110
Bryant, William Franklin, 96

Cagle, Mary Lee, 22, 39–43
Chambers, Nora, 95–100
Chicago Bible Society, 10, 12
Chicago Evangelism Society, 11–12
Chicago Evangelistic Institute, 33, 61
Chicago Training School, 7, 15–17, 25
Christ for the Nations Institute, 147–48
Christ for the Nations, 147–48
The Christian Alliance and Foreign Missionary Weekly, 90
Christian Cathedral, 132
Christian Higher Life, 81
Christian Missionary Alliance, 75–76, 88, 91–94, 113
Christian Temple, 131
Christian Union Church, 95–97
Christian, William, 123
Church of God (Cleveland, Tennessee), 96–99, 135
Church of God in Christ, 77

Index

Church of God Publishing House, 98
Church of the Living God, Pillar and Ground of Truth, 124–26
Church of the Nazarene, 21–23, 35, 37, 43, 47–48, 53
Conn, Charles, 96, 99
Craig, Mary, 101–6
Craig, Robert J., 101–3, 105

DeJernett, E. C., 22
Dispensationalism, 88
Draper, M. Anna, 28
Draper, Minnie Tingley, 90–94
Dryer, Emma, 8–12

Ebersake, Nellie Huger, 7
Elim Faith Home, 81, 83
Elim Tabernacle, 82–83
Epworth Evangelistic Institute, 31–33
Evangel (Church of God, Cleveland, Tennessee), 99
Evangel (Assemblies of God), 135

Faith Homes, 89, 114–15
"Faith Principle," 81, 115–16
Female Academies, xv
Female Seminaries, xvi
Fire-Baptized Holiness, 49–51, 96
Fliedner, Theodore, 13
Free Methodist Church, 20–21, 40, 80
Fry, Elizabeth, 13

Garrett Biblical Institute, 6–7, 35, 80
Garrett, Eliza, 3–7, 80
Garrett-Evangelical Theological Seminary, 7
Gibson, Christine Amelia, 112–16
Glad Tidings Bible Institute, 6, 94, 101, 103–5, 104–5, 118
Glad Tidings Temple, 101, 104
Glossolalia, 58

Gospel Publishing House, 120
Guide, 50
Hadley, Philena B., 25, 28
Harper, Elizabeth B., 26, 28
Hill, Mary A., 25–27, 37–38
Hoke, Mattie, 44–48
Holiness Academy, 22
"Holiness Bands," 124
Holmes Bible School, 98
Home of Peace, 76
Hutton, David L., 111

Inasmuch, 32–33
International Church of the Foursquare Gospel, 110, 131, 139, 142, 148
Irwin, Benjamin Hardin, 49

Junior Jewels, 99
Jernigan, C. B., 44–45, 47, 52
Jernigan, Johnny, 44

Kaiserwerth Deaconesses, 13
Kansas Holiness Institute, 47
Keith Bible Institute, 126
Keith, Lonnie, 126
Keith, Mary, 122–27
Kentucky Mountain Bible Institute, 63–64
Kentucky Mountain Holiness Association, 63–64
Kerr, Ruth, 65–70
Kiteley, David, 140–41
Kiteley, Violet, 139–43
Knight, Giles, 130
Ku Klux Klan, 55, 59, 111

Lake, John G., 144–45
Landmark Baptists, 95
Latin American Bible Institute, 104, 119–20
The Latter Day Saints of the Foundation of True Holiness and Sanctification, 124

Index

The Latter Rain Evangel, 93
Lewis, Felix Early, 123
Lewis, Walter Curtis, 123, 125
LIFE Bible College, 110–11, 131, 146
Lindsay, Freda, 144–48
The Lighted Pathway, 99
Luce, Alice, 77, 104, 117–21
Lyon, Mary, xviii

Mallory, Mattie, 49–54
May Institutes, 10
McConnell, Lela, 60–64
McPherson, Aimee Semple, 103, 107–11, 139
McPherson, Harold Stewart, 110
The Message, 16
Methodism, 4, 108
Methodist Church, 14, 19–20, 31–32, 34–36, 44, 47–49, 51, 53, 57, 60–61, 66, 78, 86–87, 113, 123, 129
Methodist Episcopal Church, 4, 6, 9, 13–18, 22, 25, 40–41, 56–57, 62, 81, 110
Methodist Perfectionism, 7
Meyer, Lucy Rider, 7, 13–18
Mix, Elizabeth, 73
Montgomery, Carrie Judd, 73–78, 88, 97, 104, 115
Montgomery, George, 75–77, 104
Moody Bible Institute, 11, 80, 127
Moody, Dwight Lyman, 9–12, 65
Mount Carmel High School, 63
Mount Zion Bible School, 116
Moss, Virginia E., 85–89

Nazarene Messenger, 44
"New Order of the Latter Rain," 141
New Testament Church of Christ, 42
Nyack Missionary College, 80, 88

Oakland Bible Institute, 131, 143
Oklahoma Holiness College, 52
Ozman, Agnes Nevada, xix

Pacific Bible College, 37–38
Pacific Bible Institute, 103
Pacific Garden Mission, 9
Palmer, Phoebe, xix, 45
Parham, Charles, 115, 124, 145
Patten Academy of Christian Education, 132
Patten, Bebe, 111, 128–32, 143
Patten, Carl Thomas, 131–32
Patten University, 132, 143
Pentecostal Church of the Nazarene, 21, 34, 36, 44–45, 52–53
Pentecostal movement, 49, 55, 58, 78, 149
The Pentecostal Union Church, 57
Pillar of Fire, 58–59
Pinkham, Bertha Theresa, 28
Portland Foursquare Gospel Church, 145–46
Purification, 25

Religious Society of Friends, 24
Rochester Bible Training School, 80, 82, 94, 115
Ruelas, Teresa, 120

Salvation Army, 75–76, 108–13
Sanctification, xix, 19, 26–27, 40, 57, 125, 149
Semple, Robert James, 109
Seymour, William, 58
Shalom Training Center, 76
Sharon Orphanage and Schools, 140
Shiloh Bible College, 143
Shiloh Church, 142
Simpson, A. B., 75–76, 90–91
South Chihli Mission, 27, 47
Southern Nazarene University, 22, 47, 53
Spurling, Richard G., 95–97
Suddarth, Fannie, 19–23, 43

Tate, Mary Magdalena, 123–27

Index

Third Great Awakening, 12
Tomlinson, A. J., 97–99, 135
Trail to the Tribes, 138
Training School for Christian Workers, 26–28, 37
Triumphs of Faith, 74, 76–77, 88, 104
Trust, 82
Truth, Sojourner, 122

Vennard College, 33
Vennard, Iva, 29–33, 61
The Voice of Healing, 147

Washburn, Alta, 133–38
Western Bible College, 69
Westmont College, 69
Whittier Academy, 24
Whittier College, 24
White, Alma, 55–59
Willard, Emma, xviii
Willard, Francis, 7
Woodworth-Etter, Maria B., 75, 103, 105
Woman's Christian Temperance Union, 6–7, 11, 30, 81, 85, 108

Zion Bible Institute, 116, 137
Zion Evangelistic Fellowship, 116

www.ingramcontent.com/pod-product-compliance
Lightning Source LLC
Chambersburg PA
CBHW071454150426
43191CB00008B/1347